HOPE
for the
HOME
FRONT

Books by Marshéle Carter Waddell
available from New Hope Publishers

Hope for the Home Front Bible Study:
Winning the Emotional and
Spiritual Battles of a Military Wife

HOPE
for the
HOME FRONT

WINNING THE EMOTIONAL
AND SPIRITUAL BATTLES
OF A MILITARY WIFE

MARSHÉLE CARTER WADDELL

new
hope
PUBLISHERS

Birmingham, Alabama

New Hope® Publishers
P. O. Box 12065
Birmingham, AL 35202-2065
www.newhopepublishers.com

Library of Congress Cataloging-in-Publication Data

Waddell, Marshéle Carter.
 Hope for the home front : winning the emotional and spiritual battles
of a military wife / by Marshele Carter Waddell.
 p. cm.
 ISBN 1-59669-032-1 (softcover)
 1. Christian women—Religious life. 2. Military spouses—Religious
life. I. Title.
 BV4528.15.W33 2006
 248.8'435—dc22
    2006008459

ISBN: 1-59669-032-1

N064147 • 0806 • 9M1

Dedication

This is for You, Jesus.
You are my Husband,
my Warrior,
my Friend,
and my King.

Contents

Acknowledgments

Thank you, Mark, for always believing in me, loving me, and encouraging me to never give up. I'd marry you again and follow you to the moon.

Thank you, Joshua, Jordan, and Jenna. You are cities on a hill for your generation. You inspire me. I love each one of you just the way you are.

Thank you, Mom, for introducing me to my Savior. Thank you for teaching me and reminding me that we are called and equipped to serve Him. Thank you for your endless, unconditional love and for the typing, editing, proofreading, typesetting, and support of this work. Once again, you've helped make my dreams come true.

Thank you, Jill Rhodes of Grace and Glory Ministries, for your unexpected, invaluable, timely help. Through you, God demonstrated to me Spirit-led selflessness and wholehearted commitment to our Lord. I stand amazed at how God mysteriously works to fulfill His plans. Thank you for being His willing vessel.

Thanks to all my sisters on the home front around the world. You know who you are. You are the most incredible women I have ever met! The interweaving of our lives has forever changed me and made me a better person.

I salute you.

Introduction

Hope for the Home Front explores the emotional and spiritual battlegrounds common in the experience of today's military wife. This book speaks from my personal experiences and offers scriptural encouragement to millions of others who bear similar burdens of fear, loneliness, anger, disappointment, temptation, frequent moves, single parenting, and separation from loved ones.

Demands on persons in the United States Armed Forces and their families are again on the increase. Greater demands mean more frequent and lengthier separations for husbands and wives, an exponential growth in single parenting, and an off-the-charts rise in fear and worry. *Hope for the Home Front* ministers to those who are entrenched at home in the battle for their marriages, their children, their faith, and their sanity, which are all caught in the crossfire.

My marriage of over 25 years to a US Navy SEAL has brought many trials and triumphs, celebrations and crises into my life, which all military wives understand. These experiences have become achievements that qualify me to pen this particular book, and each circumstance has taught me to trust our sovereign God more wholly.

Hope for the Home Front seeks to provide comfort and understanding to servicemen's wives and family members worldwide who are fighting unique battles of their own at home. Most are facing these skirmishes alone and unarmed. *Hope for the Home Front* arms these individuals with the power and protection of God's promises against depression, bitterness, destructive choices, and desperation. The truth, presented with humor and honesty, makes *Hope for the Home Front* a timely and timeless stronghold for its every reader. It also serves as a resource for valuable insight and ministry ideas for everyone who loves or knows a military family.

A Prayer for Military Families

Dear Heavenly Father,

I pray for every person in every place who loves, waits for, and stands behind a US service member today. These people are near to us, Lord, in our own churches and in our own neighborhoods. We pass them in our cars, in our grocery store aisles, and in our school halls and stand by them in our bank and post office lines. Lord, they are also far from us, scattered worldwide in foreign countries, far from friends and extended family, and far from the comforts and conveniences of home. Lord, You know each one, each wife, each husband, each daughter, each son, each mother and father, each brother and sister, each grandparent, each uncle and aunt, each friend who holds a service member close at heart.

Lord, my heart cries for these people because I am one of them. I feel the longings, the joys, the fears of their hearts. I've been where they are, traveled the lonely road they travel, slept in an empty bed as they do. So Lord, while it is a privilege for me to pray for these, this prayer is also a piercing that opens afresh a place inside of me that hurts with them, a secret place inside that only You know, a place in my heart and in the hearts of all who love a serviceman, a place that is sacred, solitary, protected, hidden from the rest of the world.

As compassion rises up within me for these families, I am reminded that compassion rises up in You, too. You, Jesus, our High Priest, have experienced all that we experience. You, Jesus, suffered all and more than we will ever bear. This comforts me, Lord. It comforts me to know that, though my prayer is only from one human heart, imperfect, incomplete, and incompetent left to itself, You, Lord Jesus, stand in the gap for me, interceding for these men, women, and children, who, while the rest of the world goes about its business, are standing behind our soldiers and sailors 24 hours a day, 365 days a year. You understand, Jesus, and You make my prayer for them complete and perfect as it ascends to our Father.

My prayer, Lord, is first for those who do not know You, those who do not have a true, personal relationship with You. O Lord, how they must ache and fear and drift through day after day without the real, lasting peace and comfort that come from belonging to You. I pray for their salvation. Save them, God. Work in and through the stressful and demanding circumstances in which they find themselves. Show them Your face. Let them feel Your hand on them. Let them hear Your voice. Draw them to Yourself. For there, in You, they will find life and rest and reasons and comfort that the world around them can't give. For there, in You, they will find all the resources they need to live out Your will for their lives.

I pray also for those families who serve You as they serve our country—Your people. Thank You that so many of our soldiers and their families live close to Your very heart. They are the most amazing people I have ever known, Lord. Their faith in You in an extremely difficult and demanding lifestyle inspires me. Thank You for these who doubly serve, serving You first and serving the American people second. Lord, strengthen these people. Whisper in their ears that You are near. Remind them that those who know Your name will put their trust in You and that You have never forsaken them.

Remind the lonely wife who sleeps in an empty bed tonight that You are the Bridegroom for whom she waits. Remind Your little ones that You are the Father to the fatherless and that they have a big, strong Daddy with big, strong arms. Remind all the family members that You cause everything to work together for good for those who love You, and that they truly *are* called according to Your great purpose.

Give courage where there is fear, fear of tomorrow, fear of not being able to stand under the constant demands, the constant drain of the service life. Give strength, give

Thank You, Lord, for these who doubly serve— You first and the American people second.

good health, give wisdom for every minute-by-minute decision spouses and children must make while living separated from their service members. Lord, give hope and courage to those spouses of service members who are training and preparing to ship out. The strain on these families is heavy. Make their family time and couple time sweet and intimate and meaningful, times they can look back on and draw strength from in the days ahead when their loved ones are far from them.

Lord, I pray for the loved ones of soldiers who have given their lives, the ultimate sacrifice. Lord, please be everything to those who have lost everything in the one they loved. Be glorified in bringing about Your will in their lives. I pray also for those who are yet to be widowed and orphaned in the name of freedom. God, prepare them consciously and subconsciously for this sacrifice. Thank You that You are sovereign in everything, even in those situations we do not understand and wouldn't choose.

And I pray for those who serve the ones who serve America, those friends and neighbors who can lend a hand, give an encouraging word or touch, or simply and most importantly, pray for the spouses and the children of service members. Lord, give them a new compassion, a new burden for us. Give them eyes to see the needs and hearts of love to reach out and meet them.

Lord, thank You for all who serve our nation—those on the front lines, those in leadership, those in training. Thank You for all those who stand behind them—the spouses, the children, the families, the friends. Thank You that You are near to us and near to them. Thank You that You are faithful to us. I lift them before You. I pray for Your will for them, Your tender mercies over them, and Your embrace around them. Keep those on the home front in our hearts and minds in wartime and in peacetime, remembering that *their* hearts and souls are also under fire in the trenches, in the cockpits, on the ships' decks, with the ones they love today. Bless them, Lord, and keep them close to Your heart, I pray.

In the name of our Lord Jesus Christ, who is our Victor in every battle, I ask these things. Amen.

Grateful to be anchored in You,
Marshéle

Facing Fear with Faith

i have many reasons to feel fear. I married an endangered species. My husband chose a vocation that plunges him beneath the bellies of monstrous ships and submarines and into the black depths of the sea where slimy, barnacled creatures lie in wait. He selected a profession that routinely drops him 120 miles per hour through glistening cumulus clouds from an altitude of 13,000 feet and sends him plummeting to the brown, hard earth, suspended only by the fragile threads of parachute nylon. He chose a career that requires daily expert handling of enough ordnance and explosives to ensure the success of any *coup d'etat*.

I am surrounded by friends and neighbors who have chosen equally risky professions—pilots of every type of fighter jet and assault helicopter and members of Army Special Forces and Marine divisions who train diligently and participate in real-world conflicts. My closest friends are the wives of such men. I fear the prospect of being a young widow or the unprepared wife of a paraplegic. The thought of my children being left fatherless terrifies me. I fear the same for my friends and their children.

Because my husband cannot share the secret details of his job, I fear the unknown. My best sources of world information are cable news and the Internet. I used to monitor CNN up to three times a day, depending on my assessment of the world's tension barometer, concentrating on the news anchors' every teleprompted syllable in an effort to glean any hints as to my husband's next clandestine adventure and the potential dangers he would have to face.

Reminders of Mortality

Early in our marriage, we lived in base housing on Iroquois Point Naval Reservation at Barbers Point, Oahu, Hawaii. To the east, we were bordered by the Pacific Ocean. To the west, miles of tall, green sugar cane waved in the tropical breeze. We were situated directly under the landing pattern of all military aircraft on final approach to Hickam Air Force Base in Honolulu. Several times a day, F-15s screamed over our home in exact formation. In a matter of seconds, all the hanging pictures throughout our home were knocked crooked by their thunderous vibrations. The ear-numbing shrill of their engines as they shook our house always triggered a certain pride and respect for our world's biggest and best military. But more acutely, a wave of empathy would wash over me for the wives and children who kissed those very pilots good-bye that morning. The realization that pilots don't always return home from training pierced my heart often.

The beach across the street was located on the mouth of the infamous Pearl Harbor. As a family, we spent many humid afternoons on "our" beach basking in the luscious Hawaiian sun, cooled by the ocean breeze, and hypnotized by the gentle rolling of the turquoise tide. Many a blissful moment was sobered as my eyes caught sight of an enormous aircraft carrier, a destroyer, or the sail of a fast-attack nuclear submarine as it left the safety of the harbor. I watched in silent respect as the ships glided away from their moorings, sailors at attention lining every deck like cutout paper Crackerjack dolls. Thinking of the wives and children left at the pier, the somber reminder would again grip my heart: sailors don't always return from work-ups and deployments.

The tensions that mount as my husband awaits orders in peacetime and especially during times of uncertainty and world conflict are unparalleled in civilian arenas. Mark has served through two and a half turbulent decades in every military geographic theater of operation in the world. Together we've mourned the loss of many of Mark's comrades, several of them fathers and all of them sons. I have stood on the sandy shore many times—my eyes fixed on my husband's submarine as it propelled itself slowly and submerged beneath the indigo horizon—and whispered prayers against coastal winds for his safe and quick return. I've stood on cold, dank piers in blustery downpours—a child clinging to each leg as I watched Mark's amphibious assault ships weigh anchor—and cried, unable to distinguish between the salty tears, the raindrops, and the ocean spray that stung my cheeks. In busy airports, my eyes and heart have followed countless military and commercial aircraft as they lifted and carried my husband into predawn twilight or blazing orange sunsets.

A Houseful of Ghoulish Guests

After every dreaded good-bye, I return to our home, a house once again haunted by legions of sounds and shadows assigned to my address on temporary duty during Mark's absence. The first night falls and spirits of fear whistle into my living room, escorted by howling northeastern winds through the gap under my front door where a weather strip used to be. As I pay bills and pack lunches in the expiring evening, these uninvited minstrels serenade my nerves with dirges in C minor. Each crescendo slams the tree house windows, rattles the shed doors, and sends unsettling staccato pops through the rafters, adding percussion to their ghastly symphony.

I shake off the shivers crawling up my spine, slide between the cool covers of my empty bed, and hesitantly turn off my bedside lamp. Their performance wanes, and in the diminuendo, drowsiness dulls my anxieties. As my heavy eyelids lower the curtain on their theatrics, a shadow play begins on my bedroom window miniblinds. My eyelids swing up to my eyebrows, and I gawk at the dancing silhouettes reaching, bending, and leaping in rhythm with the wind's creepy cantata. I pull the blanket over my nose, chide myself, squint my eyes shut, and pray that sleep comes quickly. My bedroom becomes the stage for a midnight matinee featuring shadowy contortionists, ghostly marionettes, and menacing mimes. They perform tirelessly until dawn, and I rise, a wreck from sporadic sleep and a ransacked imagination, to face a week, a month, or half a year of repeat renditions!

Minefields of Marriage and Family

My fears concerning Mark, my runaway nightmares, and the restless children that inevitably sneak into my bed night after night all lead to serious fatigue. The weariness invites impatience with my children. My exhaustion results in disinterest in friendships and ultimately the neglect of my health and home. I am swept away by yet another scare: the fear of failure, the fear of bombing out on this mission called military life. I fear I will fail to be a loyal wife, fail to be a patient and loving mother, fail to be consistent in a career that demands daily creativity and energy, and fail to stay committed to God's call on my life.

I fear growing apart from my husband. Training and deployments shrink our time together. Regardless of his assignment, we are usually separated. "And forsaking all others, you will cling only unto her," his wedding vows ring in my ears. Too often, I stand alone, tempted to believe I am the only commitment he forsook. I fear the day when we may pass as strangers in the hall, exchange rote pecks at bedtime, and converse only with dead-end comments about the kids and the weather.

I fear the effects this lifestyle will have on my children. Damage from the daily fallout of this demanding way of life seems inescapable. I fear the instability and insecurity that may take root in their characters as they move so often, severing cherished friendships, and live out a seemingly fatherless and rootless childhood. There was a time when I welcomed with pride my son's aspirations to be "just like Daddy." Today, this worthy desire has become a dagger within my heart as I realize my son's definition of his dad will include the word "absent." I imagine my daughter-in-law sleeping single in a double bed and my grandson fantasizing promised father/son outings as his father treads in his granddaddy's footprints of "duty, honor, and country" through adulthood. God promised that the children of noble women would rise up and call them blessed. I am afraid to say that many days my children rise and call me a basket case as I unsuccessfully attempt to be everything to everybody.

Fear Defined and Disarmed

Call it worry. Call it concern. Call it cowardice, paranoia, PMS, nerves, anxiety. Whatever the label, these doubts and jitters boil down to a defeating spirit of fear. As a military wife, I am a prime target for this crippling spirit. The more I dwell on my list of fears, the longer and more entwined the list grows. My list sprouts tendrils that entangle and strangle, threatening to incapacitate and suffocate me.

God must understand my tendency to revert to fear and my short-term capacity to remember His Word, for He repeats Himself numerous times on the matter! The terms "fear" or "afraid" are used at least 524 times in Scripture, including the fear of God and the fear of man. Some of the first recorded words of Adam are "I was afraid...so I hid" (Genesis 3:10). The world was pristine and fresh when fear, riding on the heels of the first sin, won first place in the destructive emotions we humans would experience. It is no coincidence that some of the last recorded words of the Lord Jesus are "Do not be afraid"(Revelation 1:17). Between Genesis and Revelation, God says "Do not be afraid" 44 times and "Do not fear" 60 times!

Have you ever had to repeat yourself a hundred times? I get exasperated having to repeat myself two or three times! God is perfectly patient. More than 100 times He reminds us to fear nothing but Him.

Noah Webster defined fear as "anxiety caused by real or possible danger or pain." Fear is a deceptive and lethal weapon of our enemy, the devil. He carries a quiver full of fiery darts whose tips are laced with its paralyzing poison. There is good news though! The Department of Divine Defense has issued a tried and true weapon to protect against Satan's arrows of anxiety. It is the shield of faith. God says, "take up the shield of faith, with which you can extinguish all the flaming arrows of the evil one" (Ephesians 6:16). By nature we are self-defensive. We all carry a shield of some sort, yet all are full of penetrable weak spots and gaping holes that bare our soft underbellies to the enemy—all but one, that is: the shield of faith. There is room on our arm for only one shield. Everyone must choose her own weapon.

A Worthy War to Wage

Keeping the faith can be a struggle, a downright bloody brawl at times. Paul told the first-century Christians in Corinth to fight the *good fight* of faith. This tells me that facing and overcoming fear is a worthy war to wage.

When my heart melts with fear, I flee to God. I hightail it into the mighty fortress of His Word, into the strong tower of His Name. The moment I am in His arms, I feel the poison of fear begin to drain from my spiritual veins. God lovingly reminds me that "There is no fear in love. But perfect love drives out fear, because fear has to do with punishment. The one who fears is not made perfect in love" (1 John 4:18). His Spirit embraces my spirit and teaches me, "The LORD is my light and my salvation—whom shall I fear? The LORD is the strong-hold of my life—of whom shall I be afraid?" (Psalm 27:1). "Though an army besiege me, my heart will not fear; though war break out against me, even then will I be confident" (Psalm 27:3). And again, "God is our refuge and strength, an ever-present help in trouble. Therefore we will not fear, though the earth give way and the mountains fall into the heart of the sea, though its waters roar and foam and the mountains quake with their surging" (Psalm 46:1–3).

When my heart melts with fear, I flee to God.

In the pending panic, I thrust the sword of the Spirit in Satan's face. "I am the God of your father Abraham. Do not be afraid, for I am with you" (Genesis 26:24). "Do not be afraid; do not be discouraged" (Deuteronomy 1:21). "Do not be terrified; do not be afraid of them. The LORD your God, who is going before you, will fight for you" (Deuteronomy 1:29–30). "When you go to war against your enemies and see horses and chariots and an army greater than yours, do not be afraid of them, because the LORD your God...will be with you" (Deuteronomy 20:1). "Do not be fainthearted or afraid; do not be terrified or give way to panic before them. For the LORD your God is the one who goes with you to fight for you against your enemies to give you victory" (Deuteronomy 20:3–4)!

Years of marriage to a military man have brought with them many trials and crises—all opportunities to learn to trust and fear only God. His Word tells me that, "Naked I came from my mother's womb, and naked I will depart. The LORD gave and the LORD has taken away; may the name of the LORD be praised" (Job 1:21). My husband, my children, my health, my home, and my future are gifts from God for this life only. I am learning to let go of Mark and all else that is dear to me here. The safest place for my treasures is in God's hands, not mine.

The number of Mark's days were ordained, determined before one of them came to be, regardless of whether he is a gunslinger or he sits behind a desk and pushes papers. The number and quality of all my days are equally in God's loving control. Mark's job *is* demanding and dangerous. The amount of danger he faces, however, in no way alters God's sovereignty. In contrast, it serves to keep my will on the altar.

When my house pops and cracks like a middle-aged linebacker, I nervously double-check my security system. I realize serious intruders can outwit wires and buzzers, so I call on God to unleash His secret service of brawny angels to guard my home through the restless nights.

Yet only His presence can guard my heart, so I rejoice that the Lord is near and remember that He said to not be anxious, fearful, or worried about anything! That includes danger, pain, orders, failure, the unknown, things that go bump in the night, and even death. "Do not be anxious about anything, but in everything, by prayer and petition, with thanksgiving, present your requests to God. And the peace of God, which transcends all understanding, will guard your hearts and your minds in Christ Jesus" (Philippians 4:6–7).

Paul, inspired by God, wrote, "For God did not give us a spirit of timidity, but a spirit of power, of love and of self-discipline" (2 Timothy 1:7). I believe that it is a decision of my will to release all that is dear or unclear to me to God. Each time I do, I sense God's approval and I am comforted. At times, however, I cannot muster up the faith that my circumstances require. Yet I am reassured that when I am faithless, He is still faithful. Jesus alone is "the author and perfecter of our faith" (Hebrews 12:2). Fear flees in the face of faith.

Militarese 101: COs, XOs, Cheerios, and Uh-Ohs

Mark and I lingered, embracing in the frame of our front door, warmed by the rising California summer sun, still intoxicated by our fairy-tale wedding and whirlwind honeymoon. Mark's leave had come to an end. The thought of an eight-hour separation seemed intolerable to us. Starry-eyed, we whispered sweet nothings to each other one last time, then reluctantly pried ourselves apart. Mark drove away, blowing kisses to me in his rearview mirror. Proud of my sailor and giddy with love, I watched until he was out of sight.

I busied myself tidying our tiny apartment that morning in an effort to whisk away not only the dust but also the work day that separated us. As I cleared the kitchen counters, I came to a small heap of receipts, gum wrappers, pennies, and other pocket contents from the fatigues Mark had worn the day before. Curious, I stopped to read a small, crumpled note scribbled in my new husband's handwriting: "Burn marriage license."

Burn marriage license? Horrified, I pondered the possible explanations. Goose bumps raised every hair on my body. I shivered as the aftershocks rose up my legs and spine. Only three explanations held water: (1) Mark was a KGB secret agent planted in US Naval Special Warfare and needed a bona fide American wife for a cover, (2) he was an assassin about to make his hit, or (3) he had a girl in every port and he intended to keep it that way. For the remaining seven hours, I sobbed in confusion and searched our apartment for phone bugs, minicameras, and other tools of espionage.

When I heard Mark's '66 Mustang backfire as he parked at the curb, I gathered my composure and tried to greet him with a smile. One look at him and my façade was shattered as a new flood of tears burst forth. Instead of being greeted with a warm welcome, Mark was bombarded by a barrage of whos, whats, and whys—one senseless question and incomplete sentence after another.

The words I promised myself I would not utter came screaming out: "Why, tell me, why are you planning to burn our marriage license?!"

Mark, shell-shocked but with his presence of mind still intact, gently wrapped his strong arms around my tense, trembling body. He tenderly looked into my swollen, bloodshot eyes and, with a smile on his lips, said, "Honey, that's just military talk. To burn something means to make a copy of it. I just needed to make a copy of our marriage license," obviously doing everything in his power to restrain the oncoming guffaw. Several seconds of silence followed. Shades of astonishment, disbelief, embarrassment, and then relief flushed and colored my face. We laughed away the last half hour of California sunset in each other's arms once again.

Broken Militarese Spoken Here

After training for a couple of decades, I now speak broken "Militarese." My marriage to a military man did not come with a handy Militarese-to-English/English-to-Militarese pocket dictionary, so I have had to spend much time and effort memorizing, pronouncing, and decoding this foreign language. A combination of run-on acronyms and Greenwich time translations, this Department of Defense (DoD) language has evolved into its own verbal and written expressions. Perhaps when God confused the languages of the world, He assigned Militarese to the general of King Nimrod's army as he stood baffled at the base of the Tower of Babel. Perhaps this new DoD tongue, though only in its infancy, was already replete with ancient abbreviations and difficult sundial readings.

The contents of Mark's pockets on that unforgettable day introduced me to a language not taught in any school. I have never seen Militarese 101 or Interpreting DoD 102 offered at any educational institution. It took me months not to equate CO, XO, and OPS-O with uh-oh and Cheerios. It took even longer to remember that the OIC, AOIC, NCOIC, or LCPO were human beings, not to mention my husband's bosses. To learn this military tongue, one must either be born into the race or converted by enlistment or by marriage. Mark received an embossed, sealed diploma after only six months of conjugating Spanish verbs at the Defense Language Institute in Monterey, California. I am still waiting for a certificate applauding my fluency in Militarese, arduously achieved through many years of on-the-job training.

The contents of my purse today testify to my literacy and improved comprehension: a TLA check stub; a TP from an MRE; a PX receipt; an Rx with DEERS information on the back; an ID that expires 11APR08; an LES with proof of VHA, BAQ, BAH, and SGLI from PSD; letters addressed APO and FPO to long lost friends; directions to the JAG office; and a note to remind myself that I have a meeting with the CO of NAVSPECWAR SEAL Team FOUR at NAB today at 16:30! In order to initiate my POD (plan of the day), however, I have to implement a SAR (search and rescue) mission to find the keys to my POV (privately owned vehicle) amid the mess ASAP!

The challenge lies in knowing when, how, and with whom to speak Civilian and when to employ Militarese.

If, unaware, I ramble on in Militarese to any civilians, be they family or friends, their lack of understanding is quite apparent as they respond to my verbal alphabet soup with the blank stare of an illiterate.

The Tower of Babble

This challenge parallels another linguistic switch I make daily when my husband returns home from work. After 12 hours of exclusively speaking Babese and Toddlerese, I must untie my tongue and rethink my thoughts in order to speak as an intelligent adult with Mark. For the remainder of the evening and then full-time on weekends, I serve as the interpreter between Daddy and our little ones.

My communication skills aren't exhausted here. I speak yet another tongue: Christianese. Born and raised in America's Bible Belt, I could speak southern belle believer's lingo with amazing ease at the tender age of three. Although I had no idea of the theology behind most of the terminology, I could readily rattle off the buzzwords of the faith as smoothly as any PK (preacher's kid). By age nine, I knew I was "redeemed by the blood of the Lamb"; however, it took several added years and maturity to understand that Christ was God's sacrifice on our behalf and that this Lamb wasn't the one who followed Mary to school in the nursery rhyme. My three-year-old daughter sings, "Be *exhausted*, O Lord, above the heavens." Later she will more fully comprehend what it means to *exalt* the

Lord. Presently, she thinks of "Father Abraham" as her other daddy. She, like all believers, new and seasoned, will gradually adopt a style of ecclesiastical expression, a doctrinal dialect, that only those inside the body of Christ speak *and* understand.

Christians are familiar with the Great Commission: Jesus's command to "Go into all the world and preach the good news" (Mark 16:15) and to "go and make disciples of all nations, baptizing them in the name of the Father and of the Son and of the Holy Spirit, and teaching them to obey everything I have commanded you" (Matthew 28:19–20). Too often, however, we share our faith with unbelievers in a language foreign to them— Christianese. To them, a *conversion* is still a money exchange term. They don't *redeem* anything but coupons. To them, to *justify* means to get even. A *conviction* is still a prison sentence, *grace* is something they recite at the dinner table, and being *righteous* means being totally cool.

Most Christian jargon is as difficult for unbelievers to comprehend today as the phrase "born again" sounded to Nicodemus 2,000 years ago. Like everything else He did, Jesus handled the question from a bewildered Nicodemus with dignity, gentleness, and perfection. In the cool of the night shadows, Jesus put His message in terms that Nicodemus could understand, explaining that "Flesh gives birth to flesh, but the Spirit gives birth to spirit" (John 3:6). Thus, the need for two births was clear to His teachable listener.

Son Language

Jesus taught the people about God, His purposes and plans, and kingdom issues in parables: short, simple, easy-to-remember stories that embodied divine truth, an applicable lesson, or an apt answer. In fact, His style of presentation was fulfillment of Messianic prophecy.

> *This is why I speak to them in parables: "Though seeing, they do not see; though hearing, they do not hear or understand." In them is fulfilled the prophecy of Isaiah: "You will be ever hearing but never understanding; you will be ever seeing but never perceiving. For this people's heart has become calloused; they hardly hear with their ears, and they have closed their eyes. Otherwise they might see with their eyes, hear with their ears, understand with their hearts and turn, and I would heal them."*
> —Matthew 13:13–15 (Jesus speaking, quoting Isaiah 6:9–10)

Jesus recognized that the people spoke a different language. Because their hearts were calloused and darkened, they could no longer see, recognize, or understand God's truth; therefore, He spoke their native tongue—not only a Galilean dialect of Aramaic, but the language of their hearts. To the baker, He expressed Himself as the Bread of life. To those tending their flocks, He showed Himself to be the Good Shepherd and the Lamb of God. To the disillusioned wives, He said He was the perfect Bridegroom. To the tax collector, He spoke of Himself as hidden treasure. To the weary, thirsty, and used-up woman at the well, He offered living water. To the candle maker, He was the Light of the world. To the physician, He was the Cure. To the lawyer, He was the True Advocate. To the mistreated widow, He was the righteous Judge. To the soldier, he was the Mighty Warrior. To the carpenter, he was the Door. To the gardener, He was the True Vine. To the writer, he was the Author of faith and salvation. To the minister, He was the High Priest. To the deceived, He was the Spirit of Truth. To the builder, He was the Cornerstone. To the lost and wandering, He was the Way. To the imprisoned, He was the Deliverer. To a new kingdom, He was the King.

A Language of Listening

I marvel at the beauty of God's ways. I have wondered why God sent a red, wrinkled newborn to struggling, poverty-stricken newlyweds. I have contemplated God's perfect reasoning in anointing a low-class, uneducated carpenter to engrave Jehovah's name in the heart of a splintered world. I have puzzled over why Jesus waited until He was 30 years old to begin His public work. I believe God wanted to learn my language. He emptied Himself of all His riches and rights to walk miles and miles in my moccasins.

When the government wanted Mark to learn Spanish, it enrolled him in a short course and issued him a stack of fat textbooks, but when Uncle Sam really needed Mark's linguistic ability, Mark was immersed in the language and culture completely. He was tucked away in a Guatemalan family's home for months for the sole purpose of becoming fluent. Jesus was immersed in our world for a third of a century, experiencing all and more than I ever will. Through His temptation, rejection, poverty, tears, laughter, hard work, family struggles, tested friendships, consistent faith, and commitment to obeying His Father against all odds, Jesus learned to speak my language!

Jesus's 30 years of listening should be my model. Too often I listen briefly to a friend's words of woe, then blurt out a pat cliché—"Trust God; I'll be praying for you" or "Just keep the faith." In reality, my language is foreign to my friend and my words are salt on her open wounds. If I would follow Jesus's example and listen long before I speak, perhaps I would learn the language of my friend's heart. I then would be better equipped to express comfort and truth in words she fully understands; however, learning the language of a friend's heart is costly. It requires patience, effort, and lots of precious, prized, priceless time, but that is true for any linguistic endeavor. Learning to speak Spanish cost Mark six months, one overseas move, and one cross-country move, and it cost the government $50,000. Learning military jargon, baby talk, and Bible lingo has cost me a few headaches. Learning the language of the human heart cost Jesus His glory, His life, and His all, and He did it solely to restore God-to-person/person-to-God communication.

The First and Final Word

I must discipline myself to listen to others, learn their language, then choose my words carefully. So much power and meaning can be contained in one small word. One chosen word can entirely change the course of a friend's life. Jesus's name before time began was "the Word." This one chosen Word perfectly expressed God's character, completely fulfilled His purpose, and totally changed the course of history. That's a statement worthy of burning a few copies!

Interruptions, Inconveniences, and Other Intrusions

etween beach-ball volleys, giggling, and elbowing my girlfriends next to me, I actually paid a little attention at my high school graduation. In her congratulatory speech, the valedictorian shared something I have often remembered: she said that in the Chinese language, the word "crisis" is translated as "opportunity." She challenged us to view our crises as opportunities throughout life.

Interruption Introduction

I accepted that challenge with anticipation. It made perfect poetic sense to me; that is, until I experienced the first major military intrusion into our two-week-old marital bliss. As Mark arrived home from work, I greeted him at the door with a sultry newlywed kiss. I flirtatiously led him to the small dining table where a warm meal, prepared with lots of my tender, loving care, was waiting. We eagerly pulled ourselves up to our cozy, oval table. As we bowed our heads to give thanks, a beeper rudely began to signal. Startled, I scanned Mark's person for the intruder. There it was, on his hip. Mark forcefully, almost robotically, returned his fork to the table, turned off the beeper, and began an amazing metamorphosis before my very eyes.

Mark's gaze narrowed, focused, and turned steely cold. The muscles in his face and neck began to strain and flex visibly. I was speechless. My chin dropped. My mouth hung open. My eyes widened in amazement. Mark left the table, strode to the hall, and hoisted himself up into the attic (never mind the ladder!). I quickly followed him and stood beneath his feet, now dangling above me as he sat in the open attic doorway. He operated as though he had done this before. Perhaps this was a routine drill, I thought, as Mark handed down to me bags of coded military equipment. My heart told me this might not be a dress rehearsal.

I felt a million emotions rise inside of me and not one of them was welcome. The next few minutes raced by as I watched him hastily prepare to leave. He threw a huge, black backpack over one shoulder, stopped in the frame of our apartment's front door and turned to look me squarely in the face. I was gazing into the eyes of a creature I had never met before. He slipped off his new wedding ring, placed it in the center of my palm, closed my fist around it, kissed me, and left.

Where Are Your Manners, Uncle Sam?

I can safely label this scenario as a bona fide interruption. This was my introduction into the real world of a military wife. Since that unforgettable day, my life has been riddled with similar bullets of interruptions, inconveniences, and disappointments as my husband has served the people of the United States of America.

Uncle Sam has a bad habit of interrupting. Interruptions happen to those in civilian careers, of course, but interruptions for the military family can be the size of tanks, aircraft carriers, and oceans. They range from unexpected "business trips," extended work hours (with no overtime pay), unannounced recalls to cancelled liberty, rescheduled duty, and poorly timed telephone calls from co-workers for shop talk. Whatever form they take, interruptions inevitably conjure up disappointment, hurt, and resentment—even anger. Not only must eagerly awaited plans be rescheduled or cancelled, but with each rearrangement, wives and children face hours, days, or months of going it alone without their serviceman.

Interruptions are all too common for me, the seasoned wife of a US Navy SEAL. Many midnight recalls have snatched my husband right out of our warm bed and sent him into hot spots worldwide to put out the fires caused by someone else's failed politics. These calls don't ever come conveniently during life's "commercial breaks," but inevitably during our best and favorite times together.

The ability to view interruptions and inconveniences as opportunities and the flexibility to accept them graciously are skills I am honing, but am far from mastering. I am a planner. I enjoy brainstorming and designing fun and enrichment for my family, making the necessary arrangements, and seeing it all come to fruition. My husband and children say I am "Rabbit" of Christopher Robin's Hundred Acre Wood gang. Planners, like Rabbit, however, often suffer from a chronic case of inflexibility. If it's "not on the schedule," then watch out!

The woman is the hub of the home. When, without warning, the military planners in DC shift gears abruptly, guess who has to change directions instantly so as not to grind the machine called marriage and home to a dead halt? You got it; it is the hub, the axle, the wife and mom. Forward, reverse, neutral, lower gears, four-wheel drive, overdrive. No wonder we feel dizzy a lot of the time. I am gradually learning that rigid inflexibility, the inability to switch gears when needed, incites me to words and actions that worsen and complicate already difficult situations.

My Own Metamorphosis

Early in my marriage, when faced with an interruption, large or small, my first inclination was to impatiently demand answers from Mark as to who, what, where, when, how, and why this change of plans could possibly have taken place. *Didn't everyone know that we already had plans?* As I exhausted him of any further explanation, I could smell the smoke from the sparks of anger that were kindling a white-hot explosion deep down inside of me. Usually I could contain the fire, but it always managed to seep out as searing sarcasm and unkind statements toward my beloved, inflicting wounds he did not deserve. When the frenzy passed and I was able to stew awhile, I threw a pity party for myself and mentally rehearsed for days every possible negative retort filed away in my mind.

Somehow, I thought that as Mark became more senior in rank that the frequency and the pace of career-induced interruptions would slow down and become tolerable, that the Roman candle would eventually run out of balls of flame and fizzle out, sit quietly, and cool off. It was not to be. Time and distance have only caused the rolling snowball of his career to dangerously accelerate and enlarge, threatening to smash everyone and everything in its vulnerable, quaking path.

Today, when my husband informs me of a change of plans, my initial response is not an outburst, but an unspoken, self-defensive "So what!" His announcement is just as piercing as in our earlier years, but the place it penetrates today has become tougher, or at least I try to think so and take shelter behind my thick skin, so the sharpness of his news won't hurt or cut as deeply. I don't respond verbally in shock and outrage, as I used to do. I try to let time and space be the cushions between my thoughts and my lips that want to give them a voice.

I cry fewer tears of anger these days and more tears of surrender, surrender to God's wisdom and God's ways. The pain is still there, probably more so now that much more is at stake than when we first said "I do." God has never failed me. He has remained faithful and near to me. These reminders ebb and flow like a patient tide across my shattered heart and, eventually, in God's timing, soften the sharp edges of the situation. The sun slowly breaks through the clouds again. Finally, thank God, the Holy Spirit gently speaks comfort and wisdom to my frustrated, breaking heart. He reminds me that my anger toward my husband, his commander, or even the Joint Chiefs of Staff is displaced. He shows me that I am actually wrestling with what God is allowing to take place in our lives.

I try to let time and space be the cushions between my thoughts and my lips.

As time passes, the years begin to draw wrinkle lines on our once-youthful, glowing complexions. Not one of us escapes this time artist who sketches crow's-feet around our eyes and permanent smile creases around our mouths sooner or later. Amazingly, he does original work on each of our faces, allowing the quality of our lives and our responses to guide his pencil.

My forehead, like no one else's I know, has multiple, deep horizontal lines that appear like an instant music staff above my eyes every time I raise my eyebrows. Mark lovingly refers to them as my "surprise lines" because they have been carved, deepened, and lengthened by a life full of surprises. *You're leaving when? You'll be gone how long? You don't know when you'll be back? You're headed where? To do what?* But just because life has drawn a permanent music staff on my forehead doesn't mean that I sing and dance through these crises as I would like to do.

God does not require that I take delight in my disappointments; however, He has told me to "consider it pure joy" when I "face trials of many kinds" (James 1:2). Honestly, how can I consider disappointments pure joy? The answer lies in acknowledging the sovereignty of Almighty God even in the minuteness or monstrosity of my troubles.

Interruption Interpretation

The good news is that God can use these interruptions in my life as a chance to display His glory, to work toward my best interests, and to prepare me for what lies ahead.

Romans 8:28 states, "And we know that in all things God works for the good of those who love him, who have been called according to his purpose." I believe "all" includes the wrenches my husband's employer throws into the wheels of our attempts at a comfortable routine.

If God in His powerful control laid the earth's foundation, marked off its dimensions, gave orders to the morning, brought forth the constellations in their seasons, and sent lightning bolts on their way (Job 38:5, 12, 32, 35), surely He is able to handle my daily planner. As I surrender to His sovereignty in my personal life and recognize His very real concern for what burdens me, I have no rebuttal to interruptions and inconveniences He allows.

We set for ourselves an injurious trap when we fill unseen days to the brim with schedules, appointments, meetings, and outings with the false assumption those days will surely dawn. It is wise to plan well for the future; however, when the details of those expectations become set in stone, we make ourselves very vulnerable to the sting of resentment, disappointment, and anger when our cemented plans must give way to God's chisel.

God has given us no guarantee that we will be well or alive tomorrow. He has not promised our next breath, yet we charge forward with an attitude of invincibility. Our Lord instructs us not to boast in tomorrow.

Now listen, you who say, "Today or tomorrow we will go to this or that city, spend a year there, carry on business and make money." Why, you do not even know what will happen tomorrow. What is your life? You are a mist that appears for a little while and then vanishes. Instead, you ought to say, "If it is the Lord's will, we will live and do this or that."

—James 4:13–15

Our self-made itineraries won't stand impregnable, but will be carved and reshaped by God-directed winds of change. "Many are the plans in a man's heart, but it is the LORD's purpose that prevails" (Proverbs 19:21). As believers, we ought to acknowledge God's control even in the unexpected rearrangements of our lives, be they minor, such as a child's endless questions, or major, such as a husband's unplanned, unaccompanied 12-month remote tour of duty.

All I have is the precious gift of this very moment, nothing more; therefore, I choose to live prayerfully and willingly accept God's redirections. "The LORD Almighty has sworn, 'Surely, as I have planned, so it will be, and as I have purposed, so it will stand'" (Isaiah 14:24), and again, "What I have said, that will I bring about; what I have planned, that will I do" (Isaiah 46:11). These promises must not frighten or frustrate me. There is tremendous peace in knowing God is in control of my times because God, by His nature, is all loving and all knowing. He will not cause any restructuring of my plans to harm or destroy me. He will not contradict His nature or His Word. I can find great release in submitting to God's minute-by-minute plan for my life. "He will be the sure foundation for your times, a rich store of salvation and wisdom and knowledge; the fear of the LORD is the key to this treasure" (Isaiah 33:6).

For a Christian, circumstances that seem out of control aren't. Our God is always in control. We can thank Him that He is dependable and trustworthy even when His love and power cannot be seen or felt. We have a firm anchor: our faith in an unchanging God whose promises never fail. "In you they trusted and were not disappointed" (Psalm 22:5). "Cast your cares on the LORD and he will sustain you; he will never let the righteous fall" (Psalm 55:22).

Time and experience have revealed an interesting twist: for the believer, what comes dressed as a burden is often really a blessing in disguise. A new friendship, a new skill, a new confidence, and a new discovery of truth are just some of the treasures life's interruptions have delivered. Hindsight teaches me to look at surprises, hurts, and disappointments differently. Now, instead of recoiling in anger, I find myself strangely eager to go on the treasure hunt to find the blessings God has lovingly hidden for me on the road ahead.

As I yield to His will as clay moving under the sculptor's gentle grip, I have the privilege of witnessing God's hand in motion in my daily life. He is shaping and reshaping me into an emptied, fired, and surrendered vessel for His service, with the ability to view interruptions as opportunities for good from Him.

Chapter Four

Duet Duty for the Solo Spouse

ith the phone to one ear, I scanned the dirty dishes in the kitchen sink, the junk mail and bills on the table, and the scattered toys and books on the family room floor. Mark, who was attending a training course 3,000 miles away, described his adventurous week to me. His description included heartwarming reunions with old friends, delicious dinners out on the town with extended family, and casual window-shopping on Main Street. He then asked how I was and what I had been doing. I hesitated to answer, searching for a way to make my mundane routine sound a little more exciting. How could I make insurmountable housework sound interesting? How could I describe the constant demands of single parenting as appealing? How could I answer sincerely when a powerful undercurrent of bitterness from unfulfilled dreams, untapped talent, and a blurred self-identity swelled inside me and threatened to surge through the phone right into his unsuspecting ear?

"Oh, just the same old, same old, dear," I responded, forcing a false sweetness in my voice as I clenched my jaws in jealousy of his fun. His evening dinner plans rushed our good-byes. I hung up the phone and sat alone in the dark. Lonely and overworked, I felt tears flood my tired eyes as I gave in to the weight and fatigue of carrying the load alone.

Keeping the home fires burning may sound romantic in a country-western song on the radio. Realistically, holding down the fort is an exasperating and exhausting experience for the spouse who is frequently left solo to bear burdens designed for a duet. Suddenly, she is thrust into the roles of carpenter, plumber, car mechanic, financial analyst, exterminator, child psychologist, referee, and disciplinarian. She is required to scale mountains of unfamiliar territory, already strapped, cinched, and weighted down with a backpack full of normal everyday demands.

O Christmas Tree, How Prickly Are Your Branches

I remember a day intended for holiday cheer with my preschooler and toddler. Mark was sailing the reefs and coves of the Pacific Ocean floor in a nuclear submarine as the rest of us returned home from the Christmas tree lot.

Too proud and too stubborn to ask my willing neighbor for help, I tugged, yanked and pried our newly purchased tree out of the trunk of the car. Throwing it over one shoulder, I clumsily carried it to the side yard and plopped it on the ground. I stared at it. "Okay, tree, it's you and me." I huffed and puffed, my face reddened like that of a straining shot-putter, and managed to straddle the wild, prickly green stallion. I clanged a hammer against the bottom of the metal tree stand, making it fit snugly around the trunk. With sweat beads on my brow, sticky sap between every finger, and pine needles in my bra, I wrestled the obstinate tree into the house. When it surrendered, I stood back and commended myself for mastering a "guy thing" without my guy.

The tree was leaning to the left. I threw my arms around it again for another round, rotating it until I found the side that looked the least retarded. "Job done," I praised myself.

I filled the basin of the tree stand to the brim with water and went about contentedly decking the halls and walls. An hour later, my four-year-old son and I cheerfully placed the gifts under the tree, singing "Rudolph" and "Jingle Bells" for the umpteenth time, with all the Christmas anticipation I could muster. With the last gift in place, the basin of the tree stand caught my eye. It was already empty! This was a mighty thirsty tree! My rear in the air and my head under the tree,

I reached past the gifts to once again refill the tree stand for the thirsty tree.

To my horror, the carpet within a three-foot radius of the tree was soaked! The wrapping paper was absolutely environmentally friendly—the paper on the bottom of every beautifully wrapped gift was already biodegrading.

I bravely assured myself that it was too early in the game to fret. I rescued the drowning gifts, performed CPR, marched outside to the storage room, grabbed a tube of caulking and set my mind and energies to repairing the leak. After a few smears of caulking to the base of the stand, I refilled the basin and replaced the limp, crinkled gifts. (For future reference, caulking does not repair tree-stand leaks.) Soon, *white, milky* water covered the same three-foot radius I had just blotted dry. "Okay tree," I said, "you win, but just for today." With no ideas and certainly no energy left, I called it a day. Because firs and spruces aren't indigenous nor readily available in the Hawaiian tropics, we had ordered our tree in September. There would be no replacing the tree this year. I breathed a prayer that the uncooperative shrub wouldn't die before I could find a new stand.

That we did the next day, but only after searching the crowded aisles of not one, not two, not three, but four department stores before we found a new tree stand. I have learned that there is a great shortage of Christmas tree stands in December. I marched back into the house and showed the tree my new tree stand. It shuddered at my newfound enthusiasm and determination. It poked and jabbed me in defiance as I shuffled it back outside to the yard. I pulled with all my strength and removed the leaking stand, revealing a trunk now plastered with white caulking. "O Christmas tree, O Christmas tree," I growled as I stomped over to the tool shed. Through sweat and tears, I sawed off the chalky base of the trunk and vengefully hacked several lower limbs off and finally made the new stand fit. After 48 hours, 78 miles, two carpet drenchings, two tree stands, and a million pine needles strewn in every direction, the ordeal was over. The tree was lucky not to have been demoted to a yuletide log.

For future reference, caulking does not repair tree-stand leaks.

The Christmas tree chaos fades in comparison to so many other fiascoes that have happened while my husband was away. There is one guarantee in the life of a military wife: everything that can possibly go wrong will and usually does within hours or days of the husband's departure. For instance, look what happened within the first four days of just one of Mark's deployments: (1) the car died in the middle of a lonely, eight-mile stretch of towering green Hawaiian sugar cane; (2) I discovered a ten-pound rat had taken up residence in my kitchen; (3) the air conditioner unit fell *in* through my bedroom window in the middle of the night (explain those physics!); and (4) the plumbing system coughed, gagged, then spewed forth a grotesque fountain of sewage from every sink, tub, and shower drain throughout the entire house, during which time base housing's emergency maintenance hotline stayed busy for over an hour! Then there was the morning my kitchen greeted sleepy me with a quarter-inch thick, wall-to-wall blanket of a zillion dead and dying, writhing termites that covered every possible millimeter of counter, sink, and floor space. A termite hatch had taken place somewhere nearby, and the hatchees obviously had partied hard in my kitchen. How could anyone have slept through such a massive orgy? They had hosted Woodstock II, insect style, making free love all over my kitchen while my husband was away preparing for war.

I have one question: why does none of this craziness happen when my husband is home? Life seems to stay on the same predictable plateau, day in and day out, when he is around. The moment he departs, the winds shift and gusty weather moves in. I mean that quite literally. The only ice storms that have caused major electrical power outages and the only hurricanes that have decided to move inland did so when Mark was 12 time zones away from us. As a result, I learned how to close off and warm a house with just four blazing burners of a gas stove and how to board up and duct tape the doors and windows of my house and map out the city's evacuation route.

Unlike my VCR remote, parenting has no pause button. The show goes on. I remember photographing my three children's faces up close to send to Mark when they all came down with extreme cases of chicken pox. I wanted him to see a glimpse of the "bonding experience" we had all endured for eight weeks. I also have had the dubious honor of answering *the* question for all three children over the years—the birds and the bees question. The time for discussing the facts of life arrived on the scene only when Mark wasn't.

Who Are You Becoming?

Life's everyday demands are enough for a wife who is left behind to man, or should I say *woman* the oars. Add inclement weather, viral infections, the kids' attempts at mutiny, keeping the house from falling apart, and the bouts of loneliness, and she has all the ingredients for the recipe of resentment.

I know women who, somewhere along the way, lost their soft, feminine side as a result of weathering life's storms alone for too long. They were torn from their moorings of gentle strength and feminine fortitude and are now sailing at top speed toward becoming the old, disheveled, gruff, sarcastic woman with shades on those Shoebox greeting cards. She's "over it" and lets everyone know it. I've looked in the mirror and seen that woman looking back at me more than once.

My grandmother advised me years ago, "You are the woman you've been becoming." The transformations, whether good or bad, won't happen overnight, but one day at a time, bit by bit, situation by situation. One day, we will each wake up, look in the mirror, and see what we've been becoming—a sweet old lady or a mean old hag.

Only one catalyst, one agent of change, can reverse the negative effect this military lifestyle can have on the beauty and femininity of a woman. *It is the recognition and reliance on Jesus Christ's total sufficiency for every challenge.* He is in control, even when I'm not convinced, allowing that which works for my good and for His glory. He allows the faith-building circumstances into my life so I will learn to draw from Him the strength, the wisdom, and the love I need for every situation. That includes termites, chicken pox, rats, hurricanes, and car trouble. Every contest comes with His guarantee that *He is enough*, that His grace will be there the moment I need it.

God is enough; His grace will be there the moment I need it.

One Easter Sunday, the small, eight-person group with which I sang was to provide the special music during the offertory of three packed morning services. We had prepared for weeks. I had rehearsed day and night the one line I was to sing solo. I had it down pat, or so I thought.

The congregation was assembled—gloves, bonnets, and all. Thousands of eyes were on us. The musical prelude crescendoed. I stepped forward to a microphone to sing out my one solo line. I opened my mouth and hollered, "Hark!" Then I went blank. I was wordless. The music played on. There was no covering this one up. The entire church knew I had flubbed up. There was no turning back. I just stood there with my mouth as oval as an Easter egg.

Behind me I could hear one of the male group members cuing me in a loud whisper the words I couldn't remember. With his help, unseen and unheard by the hundreds of fancied-up folks in the pews, I could have successfully sung the rest of my part, but I was frozen in fright in all my Easter Sunday glory. I stepped backwards, joining the ensemble again. We finished our piece, but I never fully recovered. Since that day, my family and I have laughed countless times about my silly solo: "Hark!"

My point is this: I didn't have to fail. My friend behind me had given me what I needed to finish well. He spoke the exact words I needed in that awful moment. I think about it now on days that close in on me, when all eyes are on me at home. If I will only listen to His still voice behind me, I will know what to do and what to say in every circumstance.

God encourages me, "Let us not become weary in doing good, for at the proper time we will reap a harvest if we do not give up" (Galatians 6:9). I find strength and rest in Him alone. Jesus said, "Come to me, all you who are weary and burdened, and I will give you rest" (Matthew 11:28).

I am realizing that I am not left alone to bear the burdens by myself. His name is Immanuel: God is with me. He has offered to carry my yoke in exchange for His, which is easy and light (Matthew 11:30). I am convinced He is aware of my needs even in the most trying, seemingly deserted moments. I know from experience that He stands ready and willing to meet those needs.

Just when I think I can't finish my solo, I hear His voice reminding me that we are in this thing together, that we are a team. I just need to listen to Him. The result is perfect harmony.

A Father to the Fatherless

Mommy, what is a pirate?" asked Jenna, a kindergartner at the time.

"Well, honey," I replied, "a pirate is someone who takes over the ships of other people…"

"Mommy, is *Daddy* a pirate?"

Her fresh insight caught me off guard. Her preschool perspective of her dad's job responsibilities was amazingly accurate for a five-year-old. Although Mark *doesn't* wear the black eye patch and the gold earring (every day), and, yes, he *does* still have all his teeth, my youngest child's understanding of her father's career captured my attention.

I am convinced that life as a "military brat" yields a unique worldview. My young children must have thought Uncle Sam was a distant relative, the all-powerful patriarch who shaped every aspect of our family life. Quarters weren't just coins, but home. The exchange wasn't a fair trade, but the store where they got everything from pencils to pants. Going to the doctor meant meeting and exposing themselves to yet another stranger because the medical staff transferred as often as we did. Daddy's office wasn't a building, but a ship, a sub, an airplane, a quansan hut, or a firing range. Dad disappeared into vacuous black holes every morning and, on occasion, reappeared after sunset. Other times, the days ran together, becoming weeks and months, and Daddy didn't reappear. Their dad's commute was also atypical. He arrived home on bikes, ferries, Zodiac crafts, C-5 ALFAs, C-17s, C-130s, C-141s, aircraft carriers, LCAC, and kayaks.

When we browse family photo albums, I determine which baby is in the picture by the clues in the background. There's a dormitory, university kiosks, and red and gold sweatshirts; that must be Baby Josh at Arizona State University where Mark used his VEAP benefits to attend college. There's white sand, golden sunshine, turquoise tide, and submarines; that must be Baby Jordan in Hawaii. And there's pine and oak trees towering over salmon-colored impatiens and azaleas in the front yard; that must be Baby Jenna in Virginia. The photos reveal a sobering fact: most Easters, Christmases, and birthdays are celebrated sans Dad. The picture feels off balance, teetering with only one parent in the frame, or more often, no parent at all because the only parent present is taking the picture.

Walk Beside Me and Be My Friend

Josh, three years old, and I, pregnant with a second child, rode with Mark to the pier that rainy morning. Our painful good-byes had been stretched over several days, prolonged by a necessary delay to repair the submarine. We were all emotionally numb. Yet more tears still found their way to our swollen eyes as we savored one last family embrace.

Josh and I sat silently in the car watching the sub's hatch swallow Mark and his green parabag. We wouldn't hear a word from him for months. We wouldn't see him again for half a year.

"I don't want Daddy to work *anymore!*" Josh declared, pushing his lower lip as far out as it would go and crossing his arms with a *"hmmph!"*

I patiently tried to explain, "If Daddy didn't work, we wouldn't have a home or food or even a car."

"Then we'll just have to *walk!*" he firmly concluded. It was that simple to him. At least, he reasoned, with no home, no food, and no car, he'd be walking beside his dad.

I think our daughter Jordan's first complete sentence was "Where's Daddy?" At two years tiny, she asked me this question at least 25 times a day for months at a time. My answer was always the same, "At work, honey."

"But *whyyyyyy*, Mommy? Where *is* he?" Answers didn't come easily, partly because at her tender age, she couldn't have understood the whole story. The truth was, even *I* didn't know the whys and wheres or the how longs, because "if he told me, he'd have to kill me."

Independence Day

The military family usually consists of one active duty person and the dependents. That's us, the dependents— a dependent wife and three dependent progeny. Ironically, *in*dependence is demanded of us *de*pendents. Every time Daddy laces up his spit-shined black combat boots and weighs anchor, Mommy must fill two pairs of shoes, his and hers, as his walk away.

Fulfilling the mom/dad role taps and exhausts my every resource. Four arms for consoling little bruised knees and small broken hearts are instantly reduced to two. Two resourceful souls and two minds filled with timely answers for a child's perplexing questions diminish to one. One of the two storehouses of energy and creativity must suddenly supply the demand alone, doubly depleted and doubly drained.

Weeks and months of fatherhood can leave a mother frazzled and fatigued. At times, I would pay anyone any amount just to answer the next kid question or meet the next kid need. General Norman Schwartzkopf said it right when speaking of his mother in his book, *It Doesn't Take a Hero*: "I think Mom would have been glad if she could have gone off to war, too.... Instead, she found herself in tedious, completely unheroic circumstances on the home front.... She found herself a single mother with a large house, three kids, and a way of life that was impossible to sustain on Army pay."

When Boys Are the Men of the House

"We're the *men* of the house," three-year-old Josh announced at dinner on an evening when Mark was home. As they congratulated each other on their greatness of gender, we all shared a good laugh.

It is true, three-year-old boys are little men in the making. It pains me deeply though to hear departing dads say to their young sons, "You're the man of the house now. Take good care of your mother and your brothers and sisters. I'm counting on you." How ill-timed and unfair that is according to my experience and opinion. Little boys are little boys. Their shoulders are not large enough or strong enough for carrying a burden that heavy. We have made a conscious effort never to say or imply that to our son. With each deployment, we have tried to give him the freedom to be and to enjoy his age and to take on only those responsibilities appropriate to his maturity.

Likewise, while Mark is underway, I have been careful not to rely on my son, and now on his sisters, as my confidants. Children of any age don't deserve the weight of adult fears and concerns being dumped into their laps, and it is not rational or reasonable to look for or expect adult counsel or comfort from a child. It is our role to listen to the child's fears and concerns, not vice versa, no matter how desperate or lonely or frightened we may feel.

A Father to the Fatherless

During fatherless times, babysitters and family members and friends are helpful, but none enable and replenish me like my heavenly Father. I run to *Him*, relax in *His* arms, and draw on *His* strength daily as I am forced to be both mom and dad. He reminds me to teach my children that only one Father is constant, ever present, and all powerful. I fall to my knees at the end of many days and through tears praise Him that, because of His promises, even a seemingly fatherless childhood will work for each child's good and to His glory. God's Word comforts me: "He defends the cause of the fatherless" (Deuteronomy 10:18) and "A father to the fatherless...is God in his holy dwelling" (Psalm 68:5).

Alone, I don't have the 24/7, around-the-clock stamina which is a prerequisite of a mother on double duty. Neither do my children have endless inner strength to live without a dad most of their growing up years...nor do I have all the answers to their whys, wheres, and hows.

God promises that "those who hope in the LORD will renew their strength. They will soar on wings like eagles; they will run and not grow weary, they will walk and not be faint" (Isaiah 40:31). That's one potent prescription for seemingly "single" parents and "fatherless" kids, because both circumstances require so much walking with endurance, running with courage, and soaring with faith over difficult circumstances. All these are ours for the asking, leather bound atop our night stands.

Woman

He calls me Woman,
Carved from the side of a man.
He smoothes harsh edges
With hands of knowledge.
He has breathed into me
The wind of Life,
Life in His Spirit,
And, oh, how I live!
In His Son, I am born of Him,
I share the inheritance
Bought with the blood
Of the Seed of Abraham.
I love Him for making me,
The completion of all creation,
The finishing touch, not the afterthought,
But the final link in His eternal chain.
What a privilege to thank
My own Creator
For making me Woman.

—Marshéle Carter Waddell

Tempted: Absence Makes the Heart Go Wander

We exchanged glances across the crowded room. His deep brown eyes caught mine more than once. Oblivious to us, the other party guests moved and mingled politely as soft music and softer lamplight played between us. We couldn't ignore the attraction. A forbidden, unseen force drew us to one another.

The chemistry between us was instant and uncanny. Our glances became smiling gazes, unspoken invitations to meet, to talk, to connect, to rendezvous as soon as possible. I hoped no one around us could read our body language, especially my husband, who was engrossed in shoptalk with some colleagues. I gracefully weaved my way, nonchalantly and slowly zigzagging through the chatty crowd. I wanted a closer look at him. I wanted to give him a closer look at me.

I had seen him several times before at other get-togethers. It was lust at first sight and we both knew it. Bells chimed, cannons fired, and alarms screamed in my head the first time we were introduced. Initially, I only thought about him on occasion. Mental images of him, tall, dark, and handsome with a winsome, white-toothed smile, crept into my ordinary days. The occasional thoughts became more frequent. I found myself hoping to run into him as I ran routine errands. I caught myself wondering if he ever thought of me. It wasn't long until the innocent and the occasional gave way to unshakable, undeniable obsession. I couldn't concentrate in conversations, nor could I focus on my work. I desired him like no other I had ever known.

Now we stood only a few feet from one another. I was afraid, sure that everyone could sense the charge of sensual electricity trying to connect us. His eyes looked into my very soul and spoke volumes in a silent, flirtatious way. I wanted desperately to get alone with him. I wanted to touch him. I wanted to hold him.

All good conscience left me for a split second. All my promises, vows, and commitments slipped out the door in one surreal, sensual moment. Faithfulness and fidelity flew out the window as I touched his hand. I led him to a place where we could be alone, where we could throw off all inhibitions and wildly indulge our appetites.

I didn't care what anyone thought anymore. I was willing to risk it all for one luscious moment with him. We slipped into an empty bedroom and locked the door behind us.

We were alone at last, breathless and giddy from our successful, clandestine escape from the boring small talk and superficial rela- tionships in the other room. He was even more handsome up close, his skin smoother and darker than I had imagined. I fingered his face. I nibbled on his ear. He smiled. My heart fluttered and I smiled back. We were inflamed with desire for each other.

All good conscience left me for a split second.

We embraced, standing at the point of no return. My mind was made up. He was the one for me. No one else would ever do.

We fell on the bed, locked in each other's arms. I madly peeled off his shirt and bit him, chewing his chocolate head in ecstatic rapture. I had been wooed and won. Peter Rabbit himself, the best looking, tallest chocolate bunny on the party's buffet table, had seduced me. I inhaled him, feverishly consuming his sturdy neck, his broad shoulders, his chest, his muscular arms and legs, and even his cute little tail! Pete and I were finally one!

I lay there on the bed in the afterglow beside his tiny tinfoil shirt. I savored his one last crumb and exhaled a deep sigh of satisfaction. After a few minutes, I reemerged from the bedroom. Flushed, I smoothed my ruffled skirt and tousled hair and rejoined the party in the other end of the house. No one would ever know of our illicit affair. We had left no trail to follow. Ours was a delicious secret.

True Confections

I love chocolate. To me, it is a delicacy. From a simple Hershey's Kiss to mile-high French silk pie, it is acceptable to me in any size, shape, or recipe, morning, noon, or night. Brownies, bonbons, and black bottom ice cream pies have soothed many a frayed nerve and sweetened many a sour situation for me. I admit, the sweet and innocent cocoa bean has struck the deathblow to every diet to which I ever swore allegiance.

Chocolate is the ultimate enticement, the choice seduction, the consummate calorie. It is incomprehensible to me why some folks are not tempted by melted fudge, Milky Way bars, or malt balls! They are unfazed by what fells me. Conversely, that which lures them doesn't get a second look from me. Nutty treats brimming with gooey walnuts, candied almonds, or desserts topped with peanuts simply don't stir me. Neither do doughnuts, croissants, cookies, or cakes, *unless* chocolate is somewhere in the name. But believe me, a chocolate

Easter bunny isn't the only temptation to which I ever surrendered.

Not all of us are suckers for the same lollipop. One woman's aversion is the next woman's attraction. We all hunger for food, but we gravitate to diverse tastes. We all enjoy entertainment; we are mesmerized by various jesters. We all need release and relaxation; we find them at the hands of different mental masseurs that we believe will knead the painful knots out of our lives. We all need to feel secure; we try to find it in our self-made fortresses of money, materialism, and the praise of man. We all need love and acceptance; we pursue all types of lovers in search of the perfect love.

Our current situation has great bearing on the choices we make and many times is powerful enough to override all the other determining factors. Military wives experience circumstances that other women can't even imagine. The frequent and extended separations from our husbands, the repeated inconveniences and life-size interruptions, the tiresome, unending demands of single parenting during training and deployments, the difficulty of severing established friendships with each move, and the challenges of initiating new companionships with every permanent change of station are the norm for us. Each scenario embodies a potential breeding ground for temptations to germinate, take root, and send out poisonous barbs into our lives.

Daily routine leads to fatigue and suffocating boredom. Loneliness mixed with an unmet sexual drive, an empty bed, and accountability only to a phantom husband leads to thoughts of adultery with a tangible someone. Being on call to growing children and blossoming teenagers 24 hours a day can lead to thoughts of leaving home, flying the coop...in any way possible, for a time or forever, either physically or mentally...*anything* for a breather and some space.

Certain temptations knock more loudly on my door when my husband is away. The absence of my best friend plus months of mental monologue make a sure equation for one thing: the temptation to turn my attention away from God and toward myself.

At this point, the enemy launches psy-ops on me— that is, psychological operations. All sorts of sordid suggestions materialize in my brain matter, temptations targeted at my weak spots by an unseen, skilled archer. The enemy sneers, *Is this all there is? You deserve more than this...more enjoyment, more fulfillment, more attention, more credit than this. Everyone else has a peaceful, beautiful life. All their dreams are coming true. Yours aren't. Look at you. You're wasting your life following that man around the world, feeding his children, cleaning up after them day after lonely day. Packing up, packing out, and unpacking is your life story. Haven't you had enough already? I know just what you need. I can offer you some better options to the boredom, the loneliness, the stresses you so piously endure. Wanna hear a few?*

A Peddler of Lies

Early in my marriage, I found myself curious to see what this peddler had in his bag of tricks. *Anything* seemed more appealing than the rigors and the disappointments of my current challenges. His sales pitch highlighted the biggies, the obvious glaring no-nos, including lust, adultery, alcohol binges, and serious contemplations of throwing in the towel—divorce.

The other wares in his bag weren't so obvious. It took more deployments and more heartbreak to learn to discern that these, too, were shams. They were the silent snares seemingly custom-made for wives of servicemen. I call them private pitfalls, *private* because they are less visible to outsiders, and *pitfalls* because they are just as self-destructive in the end.

One such pitfall is the temptation to become habitually idle. Why not? No one is looking. Mentally and physically drained from the emotional roller coaster called military life, I am tempted to simply check out. Apathy toward my children, my home, and my friendships spreads like the flu when I become idle. My enemy's goal is to numb my mind, blur my vision, and inject my thought patterns with the anesthesia of angels—fallen angels, that is.

Next, the enemy tries to fill in the gaps in my husbandless schedule with deceptive distractions and/or nonsensical busyness. He dulls or diverts me to devour me. Excessive television watching, unnecessary napping or daydreaming, and run-on telephone conversations begin to consume my precious, God-given time. The care and love for my children are quickly reduced to mere maintenance. I find it difficult to concentrate on anyone or anything worthwhile. Voices from the past beckon me to return to yesteryear and deafen me to today's cries for help. Even more so, longings for the future desensitize me to the needs of today. Living in the past or in the future floods my soul with anxiety over the uncontrollable and cheats me out of the pleasure of the present.

Another prank from his collection of bad jokes is the temptation to become the overly self-confident, I-don't-need-you-or-anyone-else Jill of all trades. What I've thought was my own competence surprised me at times. In reality, God, in His mercy, alone had enabled me. I prize my coffee mug inscribed, "Navy Wife. The toughest job in the Navy." I drink out of it every chance I get because it strokes my prideful inclination to believe I can do it all, independent of anyone or anything else; however, the dangers of self-reliance manifest quickly. My longing for the applause of man and self always turns to tears of desperation as I realize how limited my own resources apart from God really are. My own strength, patience, and motivation are too rapidly exhausted.

A fine line exists between the ability and necessity of being independent and the temptation to live independently of my God. I must constantly remind myself to stay tapped into the only true power source. It is God's grace alone that enables me to excel, achieve, and complete any worthy task. The moment I rely on anyone but Him or credit anyone but Him for the fuel to press on, I am headed for failure and burnout. The moment I credit anyone but Him for my accomplishments, I am headed for humiliation.

> *[Jesus said,] "Remain in me, and I will remain in you. No branch can bear fruit by itself; it must remain in the vine. Neither can you bear fruit unless you remain in me. I am the vine; you are the branches. If a man remains in me and I in him, he will bear much fruit;* **apart from me you can do nothing**. *If anyone does not remain in me, he is like a branch that is thrown away and withers; such branches are picked up, thrown into the fire and burned. If you remain in me and my words remain in you, ask whatever you wish, and it will be given you. This is to my Father's glory, that you bear much fruit, showing yourselves to be my disciples."*
>
> —John 15:4–8 (bold added)

A third private pitfall is self-neglect. I stay absolutely swamped just meeting the daily needs of my husband and children. By the time everyone is fed, bathed, dressed, schooled, entertained, loved, consoled, tutored, listened to, advised, reproved, assisted, disciplined, and pacified, I have no time, much less energy, remaining for myself. It shouldn't surprise me that I contract viruses easily or that I suffer frequent headaches when I routinely ignore or deny my basic needs.

The temptation to deny myself leads to self-abuse. The culprits are poor nutrition, lack of exercise, and insufficient rest; these affect my physical state. Other temptations influence my emotional and spiritual well-being, such as inconsistent or nonexistent time with the Lord in prayer and in Bible study and the absence of vital fellowship with other Christian women.

Exposing the Enemy

The Scriptures tell us that we are involved in a battle. "Put on the full armor of God so that you can take your stand against the devil's schemes. For our struggle is not against flesh and blood, but against the rulers, against the authorities, against the powers of this dark world and against the spiritual forces of evil in the heavenly realms" (Ephesians 6:11–12).

We have three enemies. Our first is our **sinful nature**, our inclination to do wrong. "For the sinful nature desires what is contrary to the Spirit, and the Spirit what is contrary to the sinful nature. They are in conflict with each other, so that you do not do what you want" (Galatians 5:17). Paul, in his letter to the Galatians, plainly listed the lifestyle of the flesh: "sexual immorality, impurity and debauchery; idolatry and witchcraft; hatred, discord, jealousy, fits of rage, selfish ambition, dissensions, factions and envy; drunkenness, orgies, and the like" (Galatians 5:19–21).

Our second enemy is **Satan**. He preys on our sinful nature. "Be self-controlled and alert. Your enemy the devil prowls around like a roaring lion looking for someone to devour" (1 Peter 5:8).

Our third enemy is **the world**. "Do not love the world or anything in the world. If anyone loves the world, the love of the Father is not in him. For everything in the world—the cravings of sinful man, the lust of his eyes and the boasting of what he has and does—comes not from the Father but from the world" (1 John 2:15–16).

Our sinful nature, Satan, and the world never have God's glory or our best interest in mind. Ultimately each is a dangerous foe against which we believers must arm ourselves. Their highest aspirations are our defeat and God's dishonor.

Engaging the Enemy

My husband is not the only soldier in this family. I, too, am enlisted in the ranks. My battles, however, belong not to this nation, but to the Lord, "For the battle is not yours, but God's" (2 Chronicles 20:15). While Mark invades tangible enemy turf by sea, air, and land, I engage the invisible opposition on my knees. Because my Commander knows how brutal the battlefield of temptation can be, He has issued combat gear, divinely designed for my spiritual, physical, and emotional protection.

Before my feet hit the floor, I am wise to dress daily for war. Ephesians 6:13–17 inventories the protective gear at my disposal:

Therefore put on the full armor of God, so that when the day of evil comes, you may be able to stand your ground, and after you have done everything, to stand. Stand firm then, with the belt of truth buckled around your waist, with the breastplate of righteousness in place, and with your feet fitted with the readiness that comes from the gospel of peace. In addition to all this, take up the shield of faith, with which you can extinguish all the flaming arrows of the evil one. Take the helmet of salvation and the sword of the Spirit, which is the word of God.

—Ephesians 6:13–17

If I hastily start my day, entering the war zone with just one piece of armor loosely fitted, unkempt, or missing, my foe will undoubtedly target the vulnerable vital part. His prowess guarantees a bull's-eye. The arrow pierces and I, a wounded warrior, am crippled, unable to stand "against the devil's schemes" (Ephesians 6:11). Then, throughout my day, I fight ineffectively, suffer multiple injuries, and frantically limp in retreat from his onslaught. At the same time, my family and friends experience heavy casualties because I am rendered incompetent to hold the line and fight alongside them.

Defeat is avoidable when I wisely clothe myself in the armor God offers. Once I have slipped on my helmet and boots, tightened my belt and breastplate, and raised my shield, I am protected from any toxic spears Satan may hurl at me. A trained soldier doesn't just stand unarmed in the crossfire. A true warrior grasps a deadly weapon and sounds the charge. God arms us for this advance by giving us the sword of the Spirit, His powerful Word, the only offensive weapon listed in His inventory.

"The word of God is living and active. Sharper than any double-edged sword, it penetrates even to dividing soul and spirit, joints and marrow; it judges the thoughts and attitudes of the heart" (Hebrews 4:12). Jesus even demonstrated proper handling of this weapon for us when He was confronted by the tempter at the beginning of His earthly ministry. Jesus met all three temptations with Scripture, the truth all believers have at their disposal. Our arsenals are full of heavenly hand grenades, godly guns, master missiles, and all kinds of almighty artillery with which we can disarm, disintegrate, and defeat all the hostile armies that flank us.

Each time temptation becomes tantalizing, I must claim God's every promise.

Each time temptation becomes tantalizing, I must claim God's every promise. "God is faithful; he will not let you be tempted beyond what you can bear. But when you are tempted, he will also provide a way out so that you can stand up under it" (1 Corinthians 10:13). I then must obey His every word and rely on Him to meet my every need. He says, "My grace is sufficient for you, for my power is made perfect in weakness" (2 Corinthians 12:9).

83

And again, "My God will meet all your needs according to his glorious riches in Christ Jesus" (Philippians 4:19).

When I haven't trusted His ability to meet my needs and met them in my own way, I have found Him "faithful and just to forgive" me every time (1 John 1:9). But the times I do choose to trust Him to meet every need, whether a need for release, refueling, or redirection, I find Him faithful to reward me beyond all my expectations. Each time I turn from entertaining adulterous imaginations, God pours out His blessings onto my marriage until my relationship with my husband overflows with oneness, excitement, and fulfillment. Each time I deny the desire to drown my frustrations in alcohol, God intoxicates me with His joy, His fullness, His presence. When I take God at His word, idleness becomes empowered productivity; dangerous self-confidence becomes a dance of dependence in which He alone is the Partner who leads.

God intoxicates me with His joy, His fullness, His presence.

As I trust God, boredom becomes blocks of freed-up time to serve others, to pursue other avenues for ministry, volunteerism, and/or continued education. God's grace transforms loneliness into the call and opportunity to grow closer to Him, to be still and to listen for His voice to comfort and guide my heart. Loneliness becomes a reason to meet and serve my neighbors and to make time for new and old friends. God curbs my sexual appetite so I can redirect the energies into penning terrific love letters to my husband, putting together outrageous care packages for him, and preparing creative, unforgettable homecomings for him.

When I am exhausted, I am learning to lean on Him, to put my head back without guilt, and to rest in the Lord. I'm learning to be very specific in my prayers and requests of Him for help and rest. Specific prayers get specific answers when prayed according to His will. When anger raises its ugly head, I tell God about it now, instead of suppressing it or exploding. In order not to "let the sun go down on my anger" and thus give Satan a foothold, I just exercise harder, praise God louder, run faster, do more weight sets, and turn up the volume and dance with abandonment to de-stress in the privacy of my living room!

I see handsome men in every direction on every US military base. Pilots in flight suits oozing with Tom Cruise appeal, Marines in those attractive red athletic shorts, and a well-built Naval officer in his choker whites win my double take. There is nothing sinful about my admiring a man's appearance or physique. Prolonged admiration, though, easily gives way to lust in the heart of a "WestPac Widow" or a geographical bachelorette. I am learning to practice a form of "chastity of the eyes" and, by God's strength, to treat younger men as brothers in the Lord and older men, no matter how handsome, as fathers, in all purity—*even those who are more tempting than Peter Rabbit.*

Rank: A Right Perspective

*h*anging pictures is the grand finale after the orchestration of unpacking in a new home. When the portraits, prints, and antique photographs are on the walls of our new home, then I know we have finally arrived. As we wrapped up one PCS, two contrasting portraits grabbed my attention. An engrossing comparison interrupted my progress.

I sat Indian-style on the floor and propped the two photos of my husband side by side on my lap. On my left was a ruddy, mustached sailor uniformed in his dark blue crackerjacks. His chest and arm were decorated with the red and black insignia, stripes, and ribbons of a salty second class petty officer. On my right was a striking, clean-shaven man clad in choker whites and adorned with black shoulder boards, gold stars, and the emblems of an ensign. The contrast of one man in two uniforms triggered a flashback.

The day of Mark's commissioning had finally dawned at Officer Candidate School (OCS). After seven years of service as an enlisted sailor and four months of OCS, Mark, a second class petty officer, was to be instantly transformed into a fresh ensign. He left one world and crossed the threshold into another while marching to the tune of "Anchors Aweigh." Amidst the fanfare and celebration which spanned 48 hours, I quietly studied my mutating husband as he floated through each ceremony, donned in his new wardrobe, eager in his new role.

His new insignia were pinned to his lapel, not to his character.

After much contemplation, I concluded that I was still married to the same man. The changes Mark had undergone were only superficial. His new insignia were pinned to his lapel, not to his character. Rank reclassified him, but his core person remained unscathed, intact, and unchanged.

The portraits slid and settled crooked in my lap, splicing the mental film that was reeling through my memory. I blinked away the trance and resumed my comparison of the two photographs. The transitional years between the enlisted and the officer photos had added a few crow's-feet beside my husband's eyes and had plucked a few hairs from his receding hairline— minor, insignificant changes in relation to the dramatic, complete makeover I somehow expected.

I held the portrait of enlisted Mark closer for examination. I pored over the photo. Images of years gone by reappeared. Mark, an E-4, and I, his new bride, were settling into our first home, a one-bedroom apartment in Coronado, California. I had noticed a young couple, who lived in the unit below us, sneaking peeks at us from behind their curtains as we returned from shopping or ducking behind the stairwell when I took out the garbage. The scene resembled a shooting gallery. The teasing targets kept flipping, ducking, sinking out of sight. When I mentioned the phenomenon to Mark, he grimaced and replied, "Oh, he's an *officer.*" My blank stare testified to my ignorance regarding rank. "Yeah, so?" I replied. He introduced me to a new term, "fraternization," which in military context meant the guys with the eagles and chevrons couldn't be buds with the guys who had bars on their shoulders. He made it clear that fraternization was unacceptable in the world of military rank. His tone of voice informed me that fraternizing, although tolerated to some extent in the SEAL teams, was definitely off limits in the regular Navy. Mark explained that officers and enlisted folks shouldn't and don't socialize. I conceded, yet remained reluctant and confused.

During the weeks that followed, Kelly, the officer's wife, and I discovered *we* were quite compatible. Soon, Mark and her husband, Mark, found they too had more in common than their names. We were drawn to each other, as true friends are, but were forced to be discreet, cultivating our newfound friendships off the base. This was my introduction to rank and its unspoken rules.

As the months passed, Kelly and I got braver and in our boldness decided to do our shopping on base one day—*together*. As we drove through the main gate, the sentry stood stiff at attention with eyes front and saluted Kelly! My jaw fell open, and I gawked at the guard as we proceeded on to the base. He had never saluted *me* before! I shut my mouth and managed to restrain myself. The novelty of receiving such an honor never quite faded. When given the choice, I would opt to ride in Kelly's car in the weeks that followed, simply to see the sentry hop to it. All the while, I was internalizing a heated debate: why did an enlisted wife's car sticker receive no salute and an officer's wife's did? Didn't I sacrifice as much, work as hard, and deserve the same respect as she? Didn't my husband serve the same country, uphold the same ideals, and pledge as valuable a life as her husband? The answer to my questions angered and nauseated me.

I put the enlisted portrait aside and admired the photo of Mark in his choker whites. I remembered the day Mark received his commission and I visited PSD to get a new identification card. In the past, clerks in the same office had acknowledged me with a "Yeah, what do ya need?" As the young man glanced at the papers I handed him, I witnessed borderline rudeness become gentlemanly gallantry. The typewritten "Ensign" switched his gears and caused his treatment of me to radically change. "What do ya need?" cleaned up to "How may I help you?" "Yep" improved to "Yes, ma'am." "Nope" became a polished "No, ma'am, I'm sorry." With Mark's promotion came two wonderful niceties: the words "please" and "thank you."

The rise in rank also elevated the temperature of cool relationships, thawing icy edges with a warm breath of life. Acquaintances who over the years had purposely preserved the wedge of status between us suddenly viewed us as worthy of a phone call, a visit, or a dinner invitation. The sudden interest made me feel like prehistoric slime that had sprouted wings and legs and evolved to an acceptable species, a higher life form. Their new approval grated against my knowledge that I had been an intelligent being all along.

The lines of sincere friendship became blurred by the promotion. "Higher ranking" wives began to subtly take me under their wings, intending to make and mold me while the clay was still fresh and pliable. In my naiveté, I did not yet see that their favor was motivated mostly by a desire to communicate their expectations of me, bridle my youthful spunkiness, and steer me in their direction with taut reins of rank. I soon learned that their attraction to me was in allegiance to the system, not to my welfare.

Relationships with wives of the enlisted men in Mark's team, even those friendships established prior to his commission, became suspect to insincerity. Many times I felt their favor stemmed from their new view of me as the little songbird that chirped suggestions in the boss man's ear. It didn't take a bird's brain to understand why sappy compliments and unusual hospitality increased just prior to Mark's writing of their husbands' evaluations.

Despite my disillusionment, I gradually recognized the need for rank, how it plays a vital role in the security of our nation. The system, with its official grades and levels, is purposely designed to create and promote order for the task of defending and preserving our freedoms. In combat situations, there must be no question as to who gives orders and who obeys them. Confusion would incite panic. Anarchy always ends in defeat.

God's Word illustrates this principle many times in the Old Testament. Gideon, a leader of Israel, obeyed the Master Strategist's orders to advance on the Midianites, an enemy army of innumerable men and weaponry, with only three hundred Hebrew soldiers. The Israelites did not question Gideon's unusual instructions to surround the camp, smash empty jars, and blow their trumpets. The sudden and thunderous commotion in the black of night incited confusion among the enemy. In their panic, "the LORD caused the men throughout the camp to turn on each other with their swords" and flee! (Judges 7:22). The Midianites' lack of orderly leadership led to their defeat.

Later, under the rule of King Jehoshaphat, dreadful armies marched against Judah. The king and the people turned to God, praying and fasting. God encouraged and instructed them to take their positions to "stand firm and see the deliverance the LORD will give you" (2 Chronicles 20:17). They did so and, while they waited, sang praises to Him. God caused the enemy to ambush itself, destroying one another; "no one had escaped" (2 Chronicles 20:24). God used anarchy to ensure the enemy's failure.

In combat situations, there must be no question as to who gives orders and who obeys them.

The inequities of rank have teetered my concept of justice. In the anticipation of being frocked an officer's wife, I somehow believed the indignity I experienced as an enlisted wife would give way to a clear understanding of and new respect for the military system. I supposed the new vantage point would give me a clear view of its virtue and sense.

I was mistaken. My new perspective only deepened my convictions. The rules and regulations that accompanied rank were often taken too far. The ligaments intended to strengthen the body of defense were pulled dangerously tight past the point of due respect and would snap, injuring those standing in its ricochet. A system designed to produce unity and orderliness, I learned from experience, could be taken past its limits, causing disunity and injurious separations between folks.

A right perspective of rank is critical to preserving the good in the system, as well as to controlling its tendency to spill into areas it does not belong. Rank must not be allowed to play the slightest role in the way we value and treat other people. Stars and stripes sewn to a sleeve don't increase the value of any human soul. Likewise, the absence of such insignia does not mean one has any less worth. A seaman recruit and his wife deserve just as much kindness and respect as the fleet admiral and his wife. A private and his wife merit as much courtesy as a sergeant major and his. The airman and his family are as worthy of a polite response as the general and his. Each deserves loving acceptance and respect simply and profoundly because each is loved by God and is created in His image.

Pomp, Pants, and Pony Shows

One morning as Mark dressed for the day, I sensed his anxiety. He was to be the ringmaster of a dog and pony show for several captains and admirals scheduled to arrive that day. I put my arms around his neck, looked deep into his green eyes, and said, "Remember, honey, the admiral puts his pants on one leg at a time, just like you." Mark chuckled and relaxed.

All ranks of personnel, from E-1 to O-10, share the same heart, mission, and vision for our nation. The only difference is in the duties assigned to each person. Rank and responsibilities differ; their souls, significance, and sacrifices don't.

The cliché "You can't take it with you" is trite but right. Once an admiral, general, master chief, or sergeant major retires from military service, he or she can no longer command the same respect from the civilian world that person once did from the military realm. Sooner or later, the reality hits that respect is earned, not assigned.

Our pastor has said that we should remember to take our "vitamin E" every day. He meant that a daily dose of looking at the *eternal* and getting our eyes off the things that pass away promotes health. *God, His Word, and people are eternal.* The black shoulder boards, gold stars, red stripes, colorful ribbons, and shiny medals will one day be placed and stored in a shadowbox. Our bodies and worldly achievements, likewise, will be laid in a slightly larger box and given back to the dust. In the end, all that matters is our love for God and His highest creation, people. Friends and family are the only treasures that will survive past the grave. A daily dose of vitamin E-ternity can do much to correct an impaired view of people.

There is no partiality with God. Christ died for the private and the general alike. He came and died to redeem the seaman, the admiral, their wives, and their children. Because He values and loves all of us equally, there should be no partiality in us. "Now let the fear of the LORD be upon you. Judge carefully, for with the LORD our God there is no injustice or partiality or bribery" (2 Chronicles 19:7).

It is God's place, not ours, to honor and lift us up. God instructs us, "Do not exalt yourself in the king's presence, and do not claim a place among great men; it is better for him to say to you, 'Come up here,' than for him to humiliate you before a nobleman" (Proverbs 25:6–7). "All of you, clothe yourselves with humility toward one another, because, 'God opposes the proud but gives grace to the humble'" (1 Peter 5:5). "Humble yourselves before the Lord, and he will lift you up" (James 4:10).

God takes interest in and works powerfully through the ones the world's system considers low, worthless, unattractive, unloveable. "But God chose the foolish things of the world to shame the wise; God chose the weak things of the world to shame the strong. He chose the lowly things of this world and the despised things—and the things that are not—to nullify the things that are, so that no one may boast before him" (1 Corinthians 1:27–29).

God does not view people as we do. A chest full of ribbons and a shoulder heavy with stripes are not impressive to Him. "The LORD does not look at the things man looks at. Man looks at the outward appearance, but the LORD looks at the heart" (1 Samuel 16:7). Only humility, faith, and service move the heart of God. "Whoever wants to become great among you must be your servant, and whoever wants to be first must be your slave—just as *the Son of Man did not come to be served, but to serve,* and to give his life as a ransom for many" (Matthew 20:26–28; italics added). In the same way, our lives are to be poured out in loving service to others, regardless of preference, position, or protocol.

Governments, rules, regulations, protocol, and etiquette are temporary. "The world and its desires pass away, but the man who does the will of God lives forever" (1 John 2:17). God wants us to live humbly in the present and keep our focus on the eternal.

I hung the two portraits parallel, neither standing taller than the other. I stepped back to admire my husband. He had achieved much in his 31 years, I reflected. I have been the wife of an ironworker, an enlisted sailor, a ditch digger, a brick layer, a college student, a security guard, a naval officer candidate, an ensign, a lieutenant junior grade, a lieutenant, and a lieutenant commander. I am not into polygamy; I have married only once. All those descriptors equal one man with many uniforms. His attire has changed through the years; his attributes, for which I married him, have not. Even if we see the day when he is elected and sworn in as the president of the United States of America, he will still be the high school sweetheart I fell in love with long before he ever owned a uniform.

Address, Please: Where You Go, I Will Go

i will need your address and phone number here, ma'am." I stared blankly at the bifocaled, gray-bunned secretary who was helping me to register our children at their new school. "Your *address*, please?" Her penciled-on right eyebrow lifted at an odd angle above her eye as she glared at me and waited for my answer.

My inability to spout an address quickly to her made me suspect and, to be sure, did not make a great first impression. With ease, I could have elaborated about our two-and-a-half-year European adventure with eloquence—how the Austrian Alps look at sunrise, how romantic the canals of Venice are, how inspiring Rome is, and how we were so moved on the beaches of Normandy. She had asked me the one question I could not answer. I couldn't remember where we now lived.

"Oh, yes, of course, my *address*," I fumbled. I knew I had one; I just couldn't recall it in that moment, nor could I remember what city, what state, or even which continent I was standing in. Some folks have trouble remembering other people's names or the correct date. I have trouble remembering my address.

We had recently wrapped up another PCS (permanent [ha!] change of station), our *tenth* move in 17 years. By my calculations, that's one move for every 1.7 years, just a few months longer than any address forwarding order and five times as frequent as the average American's transience. About the time our mail catches up to us, we pop like fleas to our next destination.

None of our moves have been easy or convenient. Whose are? All have involved hundreds of boxes, thousands of miles, and one economy-size bottle of Motrin. All have been cross-country and/or transoceanic moves, never next door or around the corner.

Moving is a way of life for military families. The Outbound/Inbound HHG (household goods) office phone number and 1,000 copies of our new orders are things we government gypsies never leave home without. Most of us roll up our bed mats, extinguish the campfires, strap our swinging, clanging pots and pans to the overloaded cart, and move on about every three to four years. That means we win the nation's Nomad Award, hands down.

Before moving vans and corrugated cardboard, we were known as camp followers, the soldiers' wives and children who moved with the army, making meals and mending men along the way. Technology has changed everything for the troops except their transience; therefore, we are still on the march with our service members, feeding and fixing them for the front lines.

Short-Timers

Prior to the actual move date, there is so much to do. There are bank accounts and phone accounts to transfer or close, newspaper delivery and garbage pickup to discontinue, and a postmaster to notify of a forwarding address. There are medical and school records to request and gather for each family member, letters of resignation to submit to employers, powers of attorney to apply for, last wills and testaments to update, and birth certificates and social security cards to locate. There are pack-out dates to schedule; flights and hotels to reserve and confirm; and clothes to wash, fold, and pack. There can also be a home to sell or rent; realtors, attorneys, and property managers to work with; ads to place; and open houses to host. The sale of our first home required that my son and I stay behind for four long months in order for the buyers to obtain an appraisal, qualify for a loan, fulfill escrow, and transfer title of the property.

During the last two weeks, friends stop by, some invited, some unannounced, to say their good-byes, each bringing color and emotion to the drab numbness of the tasks at hand. Good-byes fall into several categories: the clinging, clutching, teary farewells that rip the heart out and require a crowbar to separate; the hand-shaking, half-hugging good-bye tempered with nervous joking and awkward conversation; the regretful, wish-we-had-made-more-time-for-each-other good-byes; and the smiling, so-long waves to that elusive, uninterested neighbor across the street. Invariably, some of the dearest folks either lose track of the quickly ticking clock or they get lost in the shuffle and good-byes are never exchanged; yet with each move, I am touched by the friends who are caring and daring enough to step foot into our family's flurry.

One of the less palatable pre-move jobs is the task of consuming as much of the existing pantry collection and refrigerator reserves as we can with as few trips as possible to the mini-mart for staples (milk, bread, and eggs). Meals become either very boring or extremely interesting during that last week. Several new recipes are inevitably invented, like leftover lavosh, frozen food festive fantasia, and whatever-you-can-dump-together casseroles. I recall one meal in particular that consisted of turkey burgers on white bread with white rice served on white paper plates with tap water as a beverage. My husband hasn't let me forget it. One family we know ate Top Ramen noodle dinners for their seven last suppers before their move date.

The morning of the pack-out finally dawns, and the final breakfast of toasted bread heels, the two last eggs, and hydrated powdered milk is served. There is an eager anticipation in the crisp morning air like the quiet suspense of reading the final page of a compelling novel. The last chapter comes to an end and, with a flip of a page, the story is complete.

As the packers push our lives into two hundred 4.5-cubic-foot boxes, I am astonished at the amount of stuff we have accumulated along the way. By midday, our cozy home is transformed into a stark maze of chocolate-colored boxes and furniture mummified in brown paper. By sundown, our living, breathing home is but a shell—dead and empty.

We pile into the car and slowly pull away for the last time. A bittersweetness stings my heart. I realize that those days, those times, those memories, the ages of our children, the stage of our marriage will never be again. Some memories I cheerfully wave farewell to, and yet others weight my heart and wet my eyes as I reluctantly leave them behind. There is a reflective stillness in the car as we drive the familiar route out of the neighborhood for the last time.

New Kid in Town

There is as much, if not more, to accomplish upon arrival to a new home as there was prior to vacating the previous one. The only difference is that responsibilities switch gears and simply go in reverse. Instead of closing accounts and discontinuing services, I am opening accounts and paying deposits for services to begin. I must find reputable pediatricians, family practitioners, and gynecologists to whom I can entrust our health and our medical records. If government quarters are not available, a home must be chosen.

Finding a new church is yet another adventure of relocating. There are as many sizes, shapes, and personalities of churches as there are people on this planet. We visited 11 churches in one new area in an attempt to find a place in which we could grow and serve the Lord! Church shopping has not become a favorite pastime, but has always proven to be worth the effort.

At Home with Homelessness

We have lived in one-story motels with a one-local-channel TV and no maid service, a 49-story Hilton with 200 cable channels and complimentary room service, and every type of temporary lodging in between. I have come to appreciate our brief hotel stays that fall between each move. Dislocation, in many ways, can be a paid vacation! For a few days, there are no meals to prepare, no dishes to clean, no linens to wash, and the kids can jump on the beds until they breathlessly collapse without getting a second glance from us. A hotel room becomes one large playpen for children and a pit stop for weary parents.

In contrast, we once lived five weeks in the two-room loft of a home built in 1740 on the Narragansett Bay of Newport, Rhode Island. I can still see the black silhouette of my son standing in front of the triangular attic window as he watched a lighthouse beacon rotate and flash across the bay through the falling springtime snow. We survived on "simply heat" meals cooked in the 12-inch microwave oven and fruit and milk stored in the three-cubic-foot refrigerator. Meals were served on a wobbly card table. In order to climb into our double bed, we had to duck to avoid bruising our heads on the low A-frame ceiling.

Once, we lived in an empty house for two weeks. The transportation office had no record of the whereabouts of our household goods. I was haunted by nightmarish visions of my hope chest sinking in the depths of the Pacific Ocean, my lifetime collection of antique photographs, wedding portraits, and family snapshots slowly tumbling into a thousand undersea niches amid a dark, eel-overrun coral reef. The phone rang and interrupted my bleak thoughts. The household goods office had located our life's investment, and it would arrive in a week.

In many ways, dislocation can be a paid vacation!

For another seven days, we sat in an empty house and stared at each other. After explaining to our inquisitive kindergartner why the house echoed, we would huddle in the hallway and quietly watch a family of mice, which moved in before we did, emerge from under the dish-washer and scurry around on the vinyl kitchen floor…our nightly, prime time entertainment.

In Panama, I potty trained my youngest along with our new puppy and picked black ticks off my children's heads as we endured infested temporary housing and watched green iguanas and parrots through the kitchen window. In Germany, the five of us awaited housing in a tight, two-bedroom apartment and passed the weeks building snowmen and "sledding" on kitchen garbage bags in the falling snowflakes the size of chicken feathers.

Our third return to the States topped them all. A serious parachuting accident plunged Mark into the operating room one week before we were to move into our new home. Preexisting medical conditions and the pressure of our situation sent me into the hospital twice before we could make the house our home.

No wonder I couldn't remember my address.

Toto, Dorothy, and the Department of Defense

The old saying is true, "There's no place like home." True that is, if one *has* a home. In our case, home is where the Navy sends us. In the interim, home is where we lay our heads. It is comforting to know that Jesus understands our transience. He became flesh and "tabernacled" with us—literally pitched His tent in our campsite—for a while. He said, "Foxes have holes and birds of the air have nests, but the Son of Man has no place to lay his head" (Matthew 8:20). Our lifestyle demands frequent moves. We have a choice either to fly apart at the seams physically, financially, emotionally, or spiritually every time we relocate or to rest each time in God's peace that "transcends all understanding" (Philippians 4:7).

God tells us that He goes ahead of His children. When the ark finally rested atop Mt. Ararat and the waters had receded, God said to Noah, "Come out of the ark, you and your wife and your sons and their wives" (Genesis 8:16). God was there to meet them when they arrived at their new home. Whether it is Mt. Ararat or Iceland, I believe He does the same for all of His own.

God's Word, My Address

When asked where I am from, I have caught myself hesitating lately. Do they mean where am I from originally or from where did I just travel? With a father who served as a surgeon in the US Air Force and a husband in the US Navy, for me home base boundaries have become blurred. God knew an eternity ago our need for roots. He also knew how mobile people would become in the end times; therefore, I believe, He inspired the psalmist to write, "Your statutes are my heritage forever; they are the joy of my heart" (Psalm 119:111). God tells me that in His Word I have a heritage that will last. "Heaven and earth will pass away, but my words will never pass away" (Matthew 24:35).

In His Word, I have a permanent earthly address, a place where my mind and spirit reside in peace and safety. My body may sleep in lodging around the world, but my soul is continually at home in His Word.

I used to have a quote taped to my alarm clock that read, "The only permanent thing in this life is change." I believe there are two exceptions to this: God and His Word. No matter how many miles I travel, how many addresses I accumulate, how many churches I serve in, how many friends come and go, I have one immovable Rock in my life: God. "I the LORD do not change" (Malachi 3:6). I have a song in my heart because, "Your decrees are the theme of my song wherever I lodge" (Psalm 119:54).

Heartaches and House Numbers

Mark returned home from his workday flushed and misty-eyed. As he came through the back door, I could tell his day had been demanding and full; yet great relief radiated from him. His eyes told me that much had taken place, but just what I did not know. Wondering if he'd been given a departure date for his upcoming deployment to the "Showdown with Iraq," I asked if he had learned anything new that day. His response: "Yes, about God." *Hmmmmm*, I thought, *okay*.

We had dinner and went through our evening routine, the only difference being that Mark was laundering the desert-camouflaged cover for his body armor while I put the kids to bed. When we finally crawled into bed, he told me.

Through three people, God had led Mark to Psalm 91. While hunting, Mark's best friend, Tim, feeling burdened for Mark, had stopped to pray. God had impressed him there in the forest to share Psalm 91, though he had never read it, with Mark. When Tim returned to his home in Tennessee, his pastor phoned to ask about Mark. The pastor, unaware of God's nudging of Tim's spirit under the oak trees, told Tim to tell Mark that God wanted Mark to claim Psalm 91. The pastor was the third; Tim was the second. I, the first, had been given the privilege of reading Psalm 91 to Mark just four days before!

We had spent a predeployment, last blast weekend alone at the local Ramada Inn. On Sunday morning before we were to check out, I picked up a Gideon Bible and turned right to Psalm 91. I joined Mark on the balcony overlooking the blue Atlantic Ocean and the long stretch of coastline. I told him I wanted to read Psalm 91 to him. I did, but only through many tears that stung my eyes and soaked my face. I read the entire psalm to him and then hugged him for a long time, not realizing, not knowing that God would soon confirm to our hearts through two more people the truths in which He wanted us to find shelter.

When Mark told me how Tim and a pastor had confirmed what had begun on a Ramada Inn balcony, we wept tears of relief, tears of gratitude together, that our

God had drawn us to this specific psalm, this Biblical *address of hope*, where we could reside, live, dwell, and call home during the dangers and challenges of the wartime deployment looming ahead of us.

As we lay there in the light of one bedside lamp, I got to thinking. Our house number is currently 917. I mentioned this to Mark, popped out of bed, and looked up the corresponding verse: Psalm 91:7— "A thousand may fall at your side, ten thousand at your right hand, but it will not come near you."

This is our "address," Psalm 91:7! This is "where" God wants us to live as we go through this trial together. This is to be our *address of faith* as we are separated—he on a war front and I on the home front—both facing the unknown. I'll never look at addresses the same again.

My Heart, God's Address

Moves test my stamina, stretch my resourcefulness, challenge my faith, try my patience, threaten my marriage, unsettle my emotions, overextend my budget, and frighten my kids. At the same time, moves make me clean out my closet, reevaluate my priorities, treasure my friendships, cherish my family, broaden my mind, and balance my checkbook.

My house number, street name, and zip code change regularly, and so do those of my friends. My address book's scribbles, eraser skid marks, and Wite-Out scabs attest to their impermanence.

There is only one Friend from whom we will never receive a change-of-address card. His name is Jesus. He said, "If anyone loves me, he will obey my teaching. My Father will love him, and we will come to him and make our home with him" (John 14:23). God living in me permanently, wherever I go, calling my heart His home, is better than any earthly home I'll ever have.

One day, heaven will be my final permanent change of station. Jesus said, "Do not let your hearts be troubled. Trust in God; trust also in me. In my Father's house are many rooms; if it were not so, I would have told you. I am going there to prepare a place for you. And if I go and prepare a place for you, I will come back and take you to be with me that you also may be where I am" (John 14:1–3).

Jesus knows the address of the Father's house. Not only does He *know* the way, He *is* the way to that house. When I receive my final orders, it will be the easiest move ever. There will be nothing to pack and it won't cost the government a dime!

Family, Friends, and Faraway Places: The Sacrifice of Separation

i hesitantly stepped toward my father and put my arms around him to say good-bye. Once again our brief visit had too quickly come to an end. Pain wrung my heart as I embraced him. I could feel the ridges of protruding skeleton in his arms and shoulders, which were camouflaged by his blousing shirt. His arms hung useless and trembling as he leaned toward me and pressed his rough cheek against mine, frustrated with his inability to adequately express his affection for his only child.

It was difficult to embrace him yet harder to release him. His arms still limp at his sides, he clumsily waved good-bye with his left hand like a fledgling pathetically testing its worthless wings. The grief welled up inside of him and pushed tears into his aging eyes. I forced a reassuring smile to my lips and managed to speak: "I love you, Daddy. We'll be together before you know it!" The silenced fledgling flapped his stump wing rhythmically. I turned and left.

I would do almost anything not to cry in front of my father. I would walk away, change the subject of conversation, and sever eye contact with Dad if I felt my throat tightening and my chin beginning to quiver. If one tear were to escape, I feared the dam would burst and I would drown in the furious cascade of emotions, so I'd square my shoulders and reinforce the structure that kept the flood in check.

My father was diagnosed with amyotrophic lateral sclerosis (ALS), a killer more commonly known as Lou Gehrig's disease, and died 17 months later. With ALS, motor neurons are inexplicably attacked and murdered, strangling and canceling any neurological nourishment of the muscles. Thus, muscle tissue starves of any impulse, degenerates, and shrinks, eventually leaving the victim fully paralyzed. Medical research has yet to discover a cure for this disease, which afflicts one in 100,000 persons.

Because my husband's naval career wedged thousands of miles between my father and me, I was stricken with a different paralysis. The distance left me helpless to be the assistance to my mother and the encouragement to my father I could have been. My hands would have served him. My arms could have steadied him. They could not reach him. My words could have uplifted him but were drowned in the ocean of mileage between us. My eyes could have watched over him, but the distance dimmed my vision. My ears could have listened patiently and intently to his heart's cry, but the chasm between us rendered his cry inaudible.

My father's weak limbs were the remnants of the hands of a skillful plastic surgeon, an artist of human flesh. The hands that gracefully and meticulously sculpted muscle and skin could no longer grasp a scalpel. The fingers that once reconstructed unrecognizably shredded faces and rebuilt the intricacies of shattered facial bone could not grip a fork to feed himself. The physician had become the patient, the healer in need of health.

The physician had become the patient, the healer in need of health.

My father's body underwent a tragic and dreadful degeneration. His appearance was transformed to the point of being unrecognizable by distant relatives and friends. I tried to numb the heartache by convincing myself that my father was already dead. This person that I occasionally visited was an impostor, a stranger in my family whom I merely tolerated. Each delusion was an attempt to detach myself from the truth, like a shot of whiskey to the drunk, only worsening the pain and blurring the sober reality.

I cherished each moment with him. I would catch my heart taking a timed exposure of him. The lens of my soul stood open, allowing my memory to capture images of his every laborious move. The images conflicted with those of the past. As a child, I believed my father knew everything and could do anything. Many a Saturday afternoon, he shared his microscope and opened my world to a world unseen. He would kneel, bending forward to focus on transparent aphids through the antiquated scope. We counted colors, antennae, and eyes. He would chuckle to himself at finding one playing hide-and-seek with a blossom's pistil. On summer evenings, I would sit and he would stand in the frame of our open backdoor; we would gaze skyward together to find the constellations Orion and the Pleiades. I was unaware at the time that, truly, I was the only star in his eyes. I remember the seasonal treat of watching Charlie Brown cartoon specials side by side and our laughter as we screamed, rattling down the dirt road hill in a go-cart he had made of two-by-fours and lawn mower wheels.

I recall my teenage years with him. My choices of sweethearts often failed Dad's criteria. One night, my dad, in his flannel pajama shorts, knee socks, and Sunday shoes, angrily chased my date down the stairs, through the door, and out the garage. We shared the triumph of high school and college graduations. We shared the aisle on my wedding day.

I knew in my heart that this father still lived behind the disease that masked him. My clashing conscience wanted me to believe that Dad was already dead, yet he was still with me. I searched for ways to unveil my heart, liberate my chained emotions, put words to my suppressed thoughts, and express my love for Daddy while he remained alive.

Delta Airlines and AT&T buffered the pain of our separation at times. The visits developed into snapshots to be memorialized in a photo album. Phone conversations ended and dissolved into dial tones. I was left with only my prayers and faith in my God. Prayer was the one eternal link that bridged the ravine between my father and me. When I lifted my earthly father up to my heavenly Father, the bridge of faith carried me safely over the torrents of grief, frustration, and seeming injustice with which I struggled.

I was 2,500 miles from his bedside when he left this life. Our final conversation was by phone, an awkward monologue between a mourning daughter and her morphined, mute father.

The Red Cross and Other Crosses

In most crises that affect immediate family members, the government will grant emergency leave and provide prompt transportation for the service member to join his loved ones. Some situations, however, cannot be accommodated, such as one Mark endured, due to the timing or the distance involved. In the fall of 1981, just two days before graduation from boot camp at the Recruit Training Center in San Diego, California, Mark received an urgent message from the American Red Cross: his mother was in grave condition after barely surviving a severe automobile accident involving numerous fatalities. Half of the planet yawned between Mark and his mother. A teacher at an international school in Bangkok, she and her husband were enjoying a weekend tour of Thailand's countryside when their minivan was struck head-on by a logging truck, killing three people and critically injuring the others. The message was a sledgehammer. Mark's chest collapsed beneath the blow.

He was unaware of the Navy Relief Program, he could not afford commercial airfare to Thailand, nor could the Military Air Command flight schedule meet his needs. Helplessness suffocated his reasoning. His thoughts sped and collided as his mind grasped to recall his last words to his mother. Every assumption of talking to or seeing her again evaporated. Amid the cyclone of misinformation and panic, his isolation became an eye in the storm. Suddenly everything was crystal clear. His parents' divorce had inflicted deep wounds years ago which to that day had remained open, vulnerable, feeding off the anger and hurt he had not yet resolved. Somehow, this shock had jolted his priorities. Suddenly the resentment, animosity, and bitterness fell by the wayside. All that remained was love for his mother. He ached, hoping his last words to her had expressed unconditional love for her. In the agonizing wait for more information, he realized that words are eternal and our present lives are not. Tears streaked his face as the truth pierced him: temporary separations can, in a breath, become permanent. Death did not sting our family that autumn. Through God's providence and protection, my mother-in-law survived and actively taught again in Taipei, Taiwan.

Just ten months after his mother's accident, Mark suffered at the hand of separation again. Once more, his orders stood between him and his loved ones, this time during a joyous celebration. Jack, his younger brother, was to be married Friday evening, July 9, 1982, in Phoenix, Arizona. Eagerly anticipating the reunion with his family, Mark sent his request for leave up the chain of command. Leave was immediately disapproved due to an unchangeable schedule that assigned a 120-foot dive to Mark's Basic Underwater Demolition/SEAL class on none other than July 9. The depth of the dive coupled with the altitude of a flight to Phoenix would present a decompression risk the Navy would not allow.

Both the dive and the ceremony took place as planned, a cousin occupying the vacant groomsman

Temporary separations can, in a breath, become permanent.

position. Every mention of the occasion and every glance at their wedding portrait remind us that commitment is not always comfortable; it demands sacrifice.

A Career or a Calling?

These frustrating and frightening experiences at the outset of Mark's naval career taught us both the importance of cherishing and redeeming the limited time we've been able to share with our loved ones in his 25 years of service. Mark and I agree that his military career is presently God's call on his life. His job promises no fame; SEALs are unsung heroes. It holds no potential for wealth; the defense budget is usually on the chopping block. Mark's choice to defend the United States, her ideology, and her people was and still is his obedient response to God's directive. For this reason, I rely on God and His Word during painful bouts with separation from those I love.

To most, a career is a matter of choice. To a few, a career is a calling. A person who apart from God chooses a vocation is *driven*. One who is called is *drawn*. The former is driven by selfish ambition, propelled by a desire for position and prosperity, nudged on by mere necessity. In contrast, the called are drawn by a still, yet unmistakable Presence, summoned by the voice of the Shepherd. "The watchman opens the gate for him, and the sheep listen to his voice. He calls his own sheep by name and leads them out. When he has brought out all his own, he goes on ahead of them, and his sheep follow him because they know his voice" (John 10:3–4). God calls each of His children individually, personally, "by name"; however, He will not raise His voice above the clatter of a cluttered mind and heart. His call is spoken in a whisper, audible only to the hearts of those whose souls lie still before Him.

The moment He calls, we must obey immediately, regardless of our family ties and obligations. When the Lord told Abram, "Leave your country, your people and your father's household and go to the land I will show you" (Genesis 12:1), he promptly obeyed in faith: "So Abram left, as the LORD had told him" (Genesis 12:4). When Jesus called His first disciples, Peter and Andrew, saying, "Come, follow me, and I will make you fishers of men" (Matthew 4:19), they pulled their boats ashore, dropped their nets, and left everything to do so. James and John not only left their boat and nets, but left their father to follow Jesus (Matthew 4:22). Jesus drove the point home when a young man in the crowd said, "I will follow you, Lord; but first let me go back and say good-bye to my family." Jesus answered, "No one who puts his hand to the plow and looks back is fit for service in the kingdom of God" (Luke 9:61–62).

God must have first priority in every believer's life. Those who brush His call aside to pursue their own desires or succumb to the wishes of others or act to protect their proximity to loved ones are, according to Jesus, unworthy of God. "Anyone who loves his father or mother more than me is not worthy of me; anyone who loves his son or daughter more than me is not worthy of me" (Matthew 10:37).

The moment we surrender our plans to God and can sincerely say, "Here am I. Send me!" (Isaiah 6:8), we must also place those we care for, worry about, and love so deeply into His hands. We cannot lay down our will and continue to carry around our worries simultaneously. Worry, sorrow, and heartache are needless, heavy baggage on the journey Jesus charts for us.

The reality escapes most of us that our loved ones are not in our hands at all as we presume; however, miles magnify this truth for us who are continually called away from friends and family. We must acknowledge God's sovereignty in their lives and entrust them to His care. Paul said, "Yet I am not ashamed, because I know whom I have believed, and am convinced that he is able to guard what I have entrusted to him for that day" (2 Timothy 1:12). If we can entrust our *eternal destiny* to God, surely we can believe Him to care for and meet the needs of those we must leave behind.

Meet the Family

Not only has God taught me to more wholly trust Him, but He has also given me many golden opportunities to witness to my believing and unbelieving family members of His constant care, provision, and leadership in my life. God's intervention in the circumstances that would not have existed had we not heeded the call give me countless reasons to thank Him. I can share my gratitude by bravely crediting Him during every visit, phone call, or letter to them. Jesus said, "Go home to your family and tell them how much the Lord has done for you, and how he has had mercy on you" (Mark 5:19).

Despite today's heartaches and concerns for my widowed mother and our loved ones in other difficult circumstances, I do not fear what may happen tomorrow. I believe "God works for the good of those who love him, who have been called according to his purpose" (Romans 8:28). Because I love Him and am called to be by my husband's side and absent from my dear ones, I believe all the trials caused by our separation are intended to crown me and conform me to His likeness, not to destroy me.

The comfort in it all is that Jesus knows exactly how I feel. He left His Father in heaven to answer God's call on His life. From the instant of holy conception in Mary's womb until He surrendered His spirit on Calvary, Jesus seemingly enjoyed only one face-to-face visit with His "family," the Father and the Holy Spirit, on the day of His baptism in the Jordan River. For 33 years, He worked, persevered, loved, obeyed, and endured all of God's will for His life. Surely He understands the longing of wanting to go home! Yet He left everything to do God's will, including the One He loved most. I am comforted to know He will never require me to endure anything He hasn't already experienced.

For we do not have a high priest who is unable to sympathize with our weaknesses, but we have one who has been tempted in every way, just as we are—yet was without sin. Let us then approach the throne of grace with confidence, so that we may receive mercy and find grace to help us in our time of need.

—Hebrews 4:15–16

God gives that "grace to help us in our time of need" by providing a "family" for me everywhere we live. He promises, "God sets the lonely in families" (Psalm 68:6). Mothers, fathers, brothers, and sisters in the faith are miraculously and beautifully interwoven into the fabric of my life, each a strong cord that brings vivid color to God's design. In Rhode Island, He sent Lynda, a sister in Christ, to be warm company during March snowstorms. He sent a sister, Gerrie, to welcome me to a new neighborhood in Hawaii; to laugh, cry, and pray with me; and to yell and scream with me in the delivery room during my daughter's painful birth. He placed two sisters, Sherree and Melody, next door and around the corner to listen to me, understand me, love me, and help me care for my children. He brought Jenny, who disliked shallow conversations about drapes and diapers, but preferred soul-probing subjects that challenged my mind and fed my heart, discussed over zucchini bread and herbal tea. He encircled me with a group of ladies, spiritual "cousins," who encouraged me and lifted me up in prayer every week. In Virginia, He even provided Nonie, a next-door surrogate grandmother, to school me in the Southern traditions of baking, canning, and gardening; to lavish my children with grandma hugs and attention; and to deliver soup, saltines, and 7-Up each time one of us looked peaked.

In Panama, He gave me another sister, Julia, to crack up with, to encourage me in the three-ring circus called homeschooling, and to be my sidekick in the *fruterías*, the fresh produce markets downtown, in search of sugar cane and hot peppers. In Germany, God sent into my life many precious women of faith, who became soul mates I'll love forever and prayer partners I know I can call on anywhere, anytime, for as long as I live.

Though my earthly family is priceless to me, I now realize that it is temporal. Only God's family is my true and lasting family. Jesus said, "'Who is my mother, and who are my brothers?' Pointing to his disciples, he said, 'Here are my mother and my brothers. For whoever does the will of my Father in heaven is my brother and sister and mother'" (Matthew 12:48–50).

It is comforting to know that He has a grand family reunion scheduled. The homecoming will not be cut short by recalls or lack of leave, but will be only the start of an *unending* celebration.

Recompense and Rewards

I won't have to wait a lifetime to reap the good fruit of following God and living out His will for my life. I know this because of a recorded conversation between Peter and Jesus.

Peter said to him, "We have left everything to follow you!"

"I tell you the truth," Jesus replied, "no one who has left home or brothers or sisters or mother or father or children or fields for me and the gospel will fail to receive a hundred times as much in this present age (homes, brothers, sisters, mothers, children and fields—and with them, persecutions) and in the age to come, eternal life. But many who are first will be last, and the last first."

—Mark 10:28–31

God told Abram, "Do not be afraid, Abram. I am your shield, your very great reward" (Genesis 15:1). God gives not only His best to those who follow Him; He gives Himself. Who could ask for more?

Chapter Ten

Foreigners Focused on Forever

*A*merican soldiers and sailors live and work on every habitable continent on our planet, stationed in at least 148 countries and in five US territories. From Albania to the United Kingdom, from Armenia to Uzbekistan, from Australia to Vietnam, from Afghanistan to Yemen, from Angola to Zimbabwe, and from Antigua to Venezuela, nearly 20 percent of the US Armed Forces are protecting Americans and American interests abroad. While a quarter of a billion folks back home are enjoying mega malls, pro sports, prime-time TV, first-run movies, smooth highways, and manicured backyards, these men and women and their families live as foreigners around the globe for the sake of freedom.

As the majority of Americans happily munch lunch at a million McDonald's, a minority of us who can't hurry on down to Hardee's must brave questionable noodle stands in East Asia, browse labyrinths of crowded fruit and vegetable markets in South America, and belly up to kebab stands in the Middle East for falafel and hummus in a pita. America's motorists mumble about gas prices and rush hour while one fifth of her military must share the road with darting rickshaws in the Far East, bicycles in Bangkok, rams and ewes in Romania, bull camels in Bahrain, and lorries in London that drive in the left lane! With addresses at new latitudes and longitudes, these service members and their families must change the time on their wristwatches, the wardrobes in their closets, and the words in their mouths to match that of their host country, adapting not only their appliances but their attitudes as well.

Being paleface *haolis* in Hawaii's Polynesian, *shaka-brah*, *poi*-pounding culture at the beginning of Mark's naval career was only a tiny taste of the adventures that we would experience as a family later when, thanks to BUPERS, we became *gringos* in Panama and *auslanders* in Germany. Orders like these to overseas assignments not only required a passport, a series of vaccinations, and tedious, probing overseas screenings, they also came with the guarantee that the experience would alter our lives and perspectives permanently. Moving *across* the country was one thing. Relocating to a *different* country was a whole new ball game…an away game, that is, from the first pitch to the last run, with a completely different set of rules, referees from another league, and millions of fans rooting for the home team, *not* ours.

Scaredy-Cats, Junkyard Dogs, and Mutts

We have discovered that military families living OCONUS (outside the continental United States) fall into three categories. There are the scaredy-cats who live full of fright, the junkyard dogs who merely survive by picking a fight, and the mutts—humble, friendly, grateful ones who, with eagerness and an open mind, simply adapt and make the most of every situation.

Our arrival at the airport in Taipei, Taiwan, is a vivid scaredy-cat illustration. After an 18-hour flight from Hawaii, we gladly disembarked the jumbo jet and filed into the crowded corridors of Taipei's terminals. I held our then four-year-old son's hand and Mark carried Jordan, our nine-month-old, tow-headed daughter, in her baby backpack. We slowly began to make our way to the baggage claim area, swimming upstream against a strong current of countless Taiwanese citizens. I noticed a gaggle of older Oriental women behind us, clucking loudly in Chinese and pointing at us, the only non-Asians within miles. They pushed and shoved excitedly, cutting through the crowds between us to get to us. I elbowed Mark, and with my eyes asked him *what* they were doing. The closer they got, the louder they clucked. Mark grabbed my hand and took the lead, our walk accelerating to a trot. They did likewise and the chase was on!

I scooped up Josh and we charged chop-chop head-on through the living wall of people that loomed in our way. The little black-haired ladies weren't deterred. They stayed right at our heels all the way to the baggage carousels, where we dead-ended into a swirling pool of people and luggage. The women closed in on us, chattering madly and laughing eerily. All at once they reached for our baby, Jordan. Like an angry mother lioness, I pounced between them, roared and pawed furiously at them. They stayed persistent, reaching for Jordan, who giggled and cooed at our antics. Our blonde baby was about to be snatched away from us by female ninjas and sold by an underground black market mafia to a childless, wealthy Mongolian family and *no one* even gave our scuffle a second glance!

Some of the women reached around Mark and with an air of victory wildly patted Jordan's head. Her sparkling blue eyes widened and she smiled a toothless, gummy grin as their many petite hands rubbed her crown and fingered her fuzzy top. Outwitted and out of breath, Mark and I stared at them in confusion. Their clamor quickly calmed. They bashfully bowed over and over, thanking us, and disappeared into the sea of people. This confusing episode became crystal clear only when we later learned that it is considered very good luck in the Orient to rub the head of a blonde child. Yet at the time it happened, we were convinced we were the victims of a kidnapping ambush!

Sadly, most dependents overseas live day to day like this, as flighty felines running scared, hair on end, to dart up the nearest tree and hide from the newness and the unknown. We have found that many families stationed overseas hide on the base, seldom or never venturing past the guarded gates, content to live "indoors" with predictable concessions and commissaries, surrounded by prickly concertina wire for the duration of their assignment. We were shocked to learn of one service member who had not left the base from the day he checked in at Patch Barracks in Stuttgart until he checked out *three years later* to return to the States! His tour of duty must have felt more like a prison sentence and his orders back to the US his acquittal and release papers! When I think of all the people, beauty, culture, tradition, humor, sights, sounds, and smells of Germany that he missed, I am saddened for him. He had been handed a treasure box full of custom-wrapped, unique memories, and he never opened it to look inside, much less to enjoy even one of the gifts. Oh, if not for his

It is considered very good luck in the Orient to rub the head of a blonde child.

aversion to new places and new people, what adventure he would have experienced!

Xenophobia—the fear of strangers or foreigners—is very real. It is alive and well and running rampant on US bases overseas. Xenophobia, however, is a thief and must be stopped. This subconscious con artist continually pick-pockets and pilfers from the lives of US service members and their dependents who serve in foreign countries. His stolen goods are the countless once-in-a-lifetime opportunities and relationships that being assigned overseas offers the military family.

The second and (thankfully) smaller group of OCONUS folks are the junkyard dogs, those who are always ready to attack, ready to criticize, always distrusting of others, always self-defensive. Though they don't recognize or admit it, they are equally as xenophobic as the scaredy-cats. They simply display their insecurities by baring their teeth and growling a lot. All of us know junkyard dogs. They are the ones whose overseas experiences are retold in a negative light and who reek of pessimism. Dark, heavy clouds seem to hover over them wherever they go, drizzling and soaking anyone who hangs around very long. They snarl at learning a new language, sigh in disgust at others' enthusiasm and enjoyment, snap at respecting a different culture, and are generally killjoys.

Finally, there are the mutts, those loveable creatures who adapt and grow, keep a pleasant outlook, and actually enjoy their mixed-up condition. Mutts more readily adjust to their new surroundings. Strangers and new situations to them are only things they've not had the pleasure of sniffing out yet.

My Bosom Buddy, Butch

My favorite childhood pet was a mutt. Butch was a quarter lab and three-quarters this, that, and the other. I didn't know to whom he belonged, but because he preferred my yard and me, I considered him mine. He was the most easygoing, agreeable animal I have ever known. Any itinerary was okay by him. Regardless of circumstances, his tail continually wagged. A ready grin always graced his jaw line. His eyes were deep brown and knowing. He was a willing companion to me, adventurous and loyal. When there was danger, Butch responded with instinctive courage. When there were changes in the neighborhood gang's plans, he consented, accepting what he couldn't affect, and made the most of the situation. He galloped, his oversized ears flopping and flapping, alongside my blue banana-seat bicycle as we raced down dusty dirt roads in the summer. In the winter, he ran beside me as I sledded down the same roads, slick with ice. He was always game for a new adventure, kicking up opossums, toads, squirrels, and copperheads on our forest wanderings together. We were bosom buddies, Butch and I, for a season of life.

That's the kind of creature I desire to be and the kind of people I want to befriend when stationed overseas! I want to be a friendly, loyal, agreeable, accepting, flexible person who curiously sniffs around and kicks up opportunities for fun and learning along the way. I want to be just like Butch!

Key to Canine Contentment

I believe one way to keep a mutt-like joy in life is to maintain a love for learning. Our three overseas assignments stuffed into one decade taught me many lessons. I learned how to speak three more languages, how to make Wiener schnitzel and German potato salad, and how to drive safely (translated "fast!") on the autobahn. I learned how to barter with Kuna Indians, how to broil bass caught from Gatún Lake, how to drive safely through city riots, and how to fry plantains in Panama. I learned how to crack open a coconut, how to hula dance, and how to make *leis* with plumeria blossoms in Hawaii. I learned how to unravel the webs of European mass transit systems and how to dodge overloaded, lopsided banana trucks, sloths, and anteaters at night on unlit Central American roads.

I learned that I own way too much and so many others don't own enough. I learned to be thankful for the blessings I have. I learned that my homeland's headlines on CNN International sound a lot different when I'm on the outside looking in. I learned that the whole world doesn't love America or Americans the way I do. Some folks are still angry about events that happened generations ago. Some don't want to learn English because of the bad taste we left in their mouths. I learned there are many people, though, who are grateful to America—those whom America fed and liberated. I learned to relax and not to take life or myself too seriously. I learned there's a lot of fun out there for those willing to chance it.

Living in a Parallel Universe

Most importantly, I learned that our experiences as Americans living in a foreign country drew striking parallels *to the challenges Christians face as believers living in an unbelieving world*—parallels worthy of our time and exploration. As believers and followers of Jesus Christ, we are no longer citizens of this world, "but our citizenship is in heaven" (Philippians 3:20). We "are a chosen people, a royal priesthood, a holy nation, a people belonging to God, that [we] may declare the praises of him who called [us] out of darkness into his wonderful light. Once [we] were not a people, but now [we] are the people of God" (1 Peter 2:9–10).

We are foreigners on earth! All of us who are in Christ are only passing through this land on orders from God's Bureau of Personnel. In everything we say and do, we represent our homeland, which is heaven, the place where God Almighty is enthroned, where our citizenship is recorded permanently, and where our Savior is currently putting the finishing touches on a place He's prepared just for us.

"We are therefore Christ's ambassadors" (2 Corinthians 5:20) wherever we go, whether based stateside or overseas.

An ambassador is carefully selected, holds very high rank in his own country, lives in a foreign land, and represents his own nation and government to his host country. The word "ambassador" is from the Latin word *ambactus*, meaning "servant." As servants of the Lord Jesus, we have been carefully selected before creation (Ephesians 1:4); we are dearly loved (Ephesians 5:1) and held in high esteem by our King (Luke 12:7); we live as aliens in a foreign land called earth (1 Peter 2:11); we represent the nation called "Holy" (1 Peter 2:9); and we are the forward deployed spokespersons for the government of the King of kings (Matthew 28:18–20)! *What a foreign assignment!!* We are not *of* this world any more than Jesus was *of* this world. According to His prayer in Gethsemane (and we *know* that God answered it!), we are strategically placed here, protected from the evil one, set apart by the truth, and sent *by Christ Himself* into the world to live and speak that truth (John 17:14–18).

> *Blessed are those whose strength is in you,*
> *who have set their hearts on pilgrimage.*
> *As they pass through the Valley of Baca*
> *[or any PCS!],*
> *they make it a place of springs;*
> *the autumn rains also cover it with pools.*
> *They go from strength to strength,*
> *till each appears before God in Zion.*
> —Psalm 84:5–7

From this great geyserlike fountainhead of realization, streams of application trickled down, watered every plain of my being, and brought new life to my sphere of influence. I identified the lessons I had learned from living as a foreigner in a foreign country and then began to apply them, to put them into action on a *faith level* regardless of my physical address.

LESSON #1

Being in the minority doesn't mean you are alone.

I recognized that as a foreigner, I was in the minority. My strength didn't lie in numbers any longer. Being stationed overseas meant the next-door neighbors, the store owners I did business with, and the children my kids played with were of different background, race, nationality, customs, and language. *We* were the oddity. Every conversation and every transaction was a draining cultural and linguistic exercise. Frustrations mounted. Loneliness crept into many days.

The same happens to Christians who are brave enough to live and to work *in* the world and who choose to not be *of* it. We are tempted to think that we are alone, that we are the only one left who loves God and lives to serve Him. At a very low point in the prophet Elijah's life, he, too, felt very alone. "I am the only one left," he told God, "and now they are trying to kill me too" (1 Kings 19:14). Elijah was not truly alone because God was standing right there with him. God had great news for Elijah in that lonely moment: "Yet I reserve seven thousand in Israel—all whose knees have not bowed down to Baal and all whose mouths have not kissed him" (1 Kings 19:18).

God has promised that even as the minority we will *never* be alone. Jesus said, "And surely I am with you always, to the very end of the age" (Matthew 28:20). We are mistaken when we conclude that we are the only one left who is devoted to God. He always preserves a group of believers called a remnant. He knows we need folks of like faith and like mind. He knows we need the encouragement and refreshment that come from relationships with other Christians. An awesome discovery I've made is that these remnants are in every nation of the world. Whether at home or overseas, we can pray to link up with other believers. God will orchestrate it in His perfect measure of time. Interestingly, it was right after Elijah's lowest, loneliest moment that God brought Elisha into his life, a man who became his successor and his "son" in the Lord (2 Kings 2). As long as God is in it, our lowest, loneliest points can be the prelude to a great big blessing. Remember this when feeling outnumbered.

LESSON #2
Listen well and speak clearly.

I learned that making the effort to speak the country's language went a long way in making and building relationships with the people. Even though I made good comedienne material as I tried to roll my tongue and gurgle my throat like the locals, my wholehearted attempts won their respect and their loyalty most of the time—that is, except the time I exclaimed, *"Estoy embarazada!"* ("I'm pregnant!") to a Panamanian woman when I meant to say "I'm embarrassed!" You better believe I was! Another faux pas was the time I exclaimed, *"Ich bin kalt!"* for "I am cold." My German friend gently explained to me that the sentence structured that way meant I was sexually frigid. Oops.

These slipups of syntax and slang and many more like them drove home the truths we've already explored back in chapter 2, "Militarese 101." As "strangers in this world," we need to know and speak the language of those to whom the light of Christ shines through us. Usually that means shelving our Christianese and being willing to stay within a context that our unbelieving family, friends, and neighbors understand.

LESSON #3
Citizenship is a choice,
a privilege, and a trust.

When we lived overseas, we rightfully retained our American citizenship. We didn't mutate into Panamanians in Panama or into Germans in Germany; rather, we valued our birthright as American citizens and kept careful tabs on the whereabouts of our priceless passports.

We were advised to blend in with the locals, to dress in culturally appropriate clothing, to use English softly and sparingly in public places, and not to blazon our American pride in ways that would be considered grossly arrogant. For the sake of safety, we modified our mannerisms, shifted our schedules, and selected our outfits to respect their customs. We did not, however, stop being Americans. Our birthright and core loyalties never changed.

Dual citizenship is allowed in a few countries. In most cases, during adolescence, the individual with dual citizenship must choose which of the two countries he will call his home. This decision was a difficult one for a young German we knew, who on his eighteenth birthday, had to choose his allegiance, submit the paperwork, and make only one citizenship official. Both the US, where he was born, and Germany, where he'd grown up, offered him many advantages and opportunities, but legally, upon his entrance into adulthood, he could be a citizen of only one country.

The same is true on a faith level. We all reach a time when we must choose between God's kingdom and the kingdom of this world. Dual citizenship is not an option. All must choose between holding citizenship in heaven or carrying the passport of this planet. As Christians, we must remember our birthright and treasure our heavenly citizenship as we complete our earthly assignments.

LESSON #4
*Keep the home fires burning
in your children's hearts.*

Living overseas with three children tripled our fun. It also taught me the importance of reminding them often of their homeland and where our loyalties are. Because our youngest had celebrated five of her nine birthdays on foreign soil, America, the land of her birth and citizenship, and its customs were vague memories to her at best. She frequently asked questions about the US, its glories, its struggles, and her loved ones who lived there. When it was finally time to return to the States, she understandably wrestled with fears of the unknown and the unfamiliar.

As Christians, we have the God-given responsibility to our children of passing on information about our heavenly home, such as who lives there and exactly how to get there. We are entrusted with the stewardship of modeling our homeland's ways and customs for our children to learn and to imitate. We are also commanded to introduce them to our presiding governor, Jesus, so they can have personal knowledge of and lifelong rapport with Him. When it's time for them to go home, they will wrestle with fewer fears of the unknown and the unfamiliar.

LESSON #5
Homesickness is a good sign.

Homesickness is inevitable when living overseas, but it is a good thing. It is evidence that our hearts are somewhere else. The same is true for us who are not at home in this world. The longer we walk with our God and the more we think about His Word and His ways and spend time talking with Him, we will have an increasing desire to be where He is. This beautiful, holy homesickness shines only in the eyes of those whose treasures are in heaven.

LESSON #6

Travel light—you're just passing through.

We had the privilege of celebrating a Jewish holiday, the Feast of Tabernacles, in Jerusalem while living in Europe. Every autumn the Jews celebrate the giving of the Mosaic Law and God's faithfulness to them during their 40 years of wilderness survival in the desert. Every Jewish family, hotel, and restaurant builds *sukkot*, outdoor booths, tents, or shelters, under which the people eat all their meals for eight days. This reminds them of God's provision during their forefathers' homelessness and scarcity of water and food in the desert.

We spent the weeklong celebration praising Jesus Christ, the fulfillment of the Feast of Tabernacles, who "tabernacled" with us, who was the "tent" of God's presence among us for 33 years, who "passed through" on His way to the cross, and who taught us to trust God's provision as we follow Him. We celebrated this Christ-centered Feast of Booths with Christians from 120 nations and the Christian Embassy.

All the emphasis on treks and temporary shelters underscored the truth that we, too, are just passing through this place called earth. We, too, are destined for a Promised Land, our eternal home in heaven. We are to travel light, yoked with Christ, until we arrive safely home.

LESSON #7
Hold hands and stick together.

Military families stationed together in foreign countries learn to form meaningful friendships quickly. There's no time to waste. Our time in-country is short and we *need* each other. Pride and pettiness fall by the wayside and folks get on with the business of being good neighbors. Issues of race, origin, status, and denomination dissipate and lose their power to divide folks who together are facing the challenges of living overseas.

The same should be true of any community of believers. We are in this thing together. Our time here is brief, and we *need* each other. We need to stop grumbling and guarding our anonymity and get on with the business of being neighbors to each other in the biblical sense.

LESSON #8
Always know where to run.

Always know where the embassy is located. American bases overseas are considered American soil. They are built and equipped to be self-sufficient for long periods of time during heightened threat. Because we did not always live on base, we had to know where to go in a crisis. We kept the telephone numbers, addresses, and maps to the American Embassy on hand wherever we lived or traveled. An embassy is a building that contains the offices of the ambassador to that country and his or her staff and is also considered sovereign soil. It is a place of security, refuge, asylum, and escape for all citizens of the country it represents. The sentries on duty there will shield and insulate the ones needing cover.

The church, the local body of believers in Jesus Christ, is the Christian's embassy in this world. We are to shield and shelter one another in crises and in times of heightened threat. We are to intercede with our home of record on behalf of those who need protection from the outside. We need to be a living, breathing "place" of comfort and security for all who seek freedom. We are to cushion one another from the crushing crowds and to be the harbor of safety for those who need cover from the storm.

Once inside an embassy, a person is safe and considered off-limits to all those who angrily surround the building in pursuit of him. The same is true of those who are *in* Christ. Jesus promised us, "on this rock I will build my church, and the gates of Hades will not overcome it" (Matthew 16:18). The Lord offers many great promises for our safety and protection, such as "'Because he loves me,' says the LORD, 'I will rescue him; I will protect him, for he acknowledges my name'" (Psalm 91:14) and "no weapon forged against you will prevail…. This is the heritage of the servants of the LORD, and this is their vindication from me" (Isaiah 54:17).

Being a stranger in strange lands taught me much about how to live faithfully *in* the world and not *of* the world. I am learning to live my life as a foreigner focused on forever.

Military Marriage: Mission Possible, Staying Together Apart

though Mark had not formally proposed yet, marriage was a bright sun rising on our horizon. A new day was dawning for us, the day when *you* and *I* would become *we*, and *his* and *hers* would become *ours*. I wanted a special place to have and to hold the necessities and heirlooms that I was collecting and would one day use and enjoy in *our* new home.

To Have and to Hold

My father and I went shopping and returned home with a sturdy new hope chest. Its exterior was made of golden oak lavished with lacquer that gave it a glossy shine. The heavy lid opened gracefully to reveal a cedar-lined interior, deep and ready for storage. Each time I opened it, the chest exhaled a sweet breath, the perfume of the heart of a ruddy evergreen. I'd lean in, close my eyes, inhale as much as my lungs could contain, exhale slowly, and then open my eyes again, invigorated by its rugged, woodsy cologne. I'd run my fingertips across its smoothly sanded cavity with a tentative touch, looking ahead to the fairy tale of married life.

During the long months of waiting for Mark to pop the question, the hope chest's vacant hollow became a crammed cradle filled with my ever-growing homemaking kit. Laden with silverware, linens, and lace, it bulged to the brim with blankets, cookbooks, and brides' magazines.

Everything Mark and I could possibly ever need as Mr. and Mrs., I believed, was packed into that hope chest. Its fullness made closing it a full-body experience that required me to sit on it and bounce until the latch caught and clicked.

From This Day Forward

Prepared and well equipped, I waited patiently for Mark to propose. He did, and the following year my navy man and I tied the knot. We sailed to our first home in a rented U-Haul truck without air-conditioning across the Sonoran Desert in June heat. Pink and white bows left over from our wedding and a white poster board announcing "Just

Married!" adorned the truck and flapped in the hot, arid wind. Destination: San Diego.

People in sports cars and 18-wheelers traveling west on I-10 with us approached the truck in the passing lane, honking and beeping their horns, giving hearty congratulations to us. Their glee turned to gasps when they got their first glimpse of the newlyweds. Mark and his fishing buddy, Phil, sat wilting in the overheated cab, braving the desert without air conditioning, while Phil's wife, Nancy, and I followed in the cool comfort of my car behind them. The hilarious scene repeated itself for 360 miles all the way to the front door of our first home. Hot and humiliated, Mark and Phil opened the back of the truck where my hope chest waited.

The task of heaving it up a flight of stairs and into our tiny apartment took every bit of their brawn and biceps. Once it was situated, I took over. I was Mary Poppins, practically perfect in every way, and the hope chest was my carpetbag. I lifted item after item after item out of the deep chest and began to happily set up my practically perfect house.

Eight years, three babies, five moves, and countless deployments later, our neat little love nest had become a mess due to lots of ruffled feathers, regurgitation, and the raging storms of real life. I puffed my bangs out of my eyes and dusted my treasured hope chest that now doubled as a table for folding laundry and a desk for typing. I paused to peek inside. Its contents had changed. A wedding album; baby booties, obituaries of departed loved ones, and newspaper clippings of wars and other world events that had involved my husband now filled it. A cedar box that had once held things for building an ideal future now held yellowing photos and newsprint that spoke of a real past. *When had I stopped looking forward?* I thought, *at what point did my sense of hope for tomorrow turn into a longing for yesterday?*

Life on the outside of the hope chest had changed for us, too. Practical flatware and dinnerware had long since replaced the silverware. Plastic place mats were our nightly linens, and sippy cups were our crystal goblets. I had last seen my sexy, silky nightgown somewhere between Newport and Honolulu. No bother though, for now I slept without Mark most nights—and in his baggy, hand-me-down sweats, for that matter, sandwiched between big brother and baby sister and a diapered baby with her permanently attached bottle.

I had promised to have and to hold Mark from our first day forward, but because he was constantly forward, having and holding him became a rare treat. Simple math showed that in one decade Mark had been home less than three years. That means that three days out of four, I stoked the home fires alone, praying for his safe and soon return, and raised the children he was home only long enough to father.

At creation, "The LORD God said, 'It is not good for the man to be alone'" (Genesis 2:18). It's not wonderful for the *woman* either while her man is traveling all over God's creation! There were and still are many days when

I echo what I heard one exasperated woman declare: "*I* need a wife!" God made a suitable helper for Adam that day. Most days the only helper I had was the hamburger kind.

For Better or for Worse

The better days were the ones when no one had a virus, when visitors came for dinner, and when everyone got to bed on time. The better days were also the days when the mailman delivered a letter from Mark. Simply walking to my mailbox was a highlight of my day filled with anticipation and hope. Mark numbered his letters to insure that I would open and read them in the order he had written them. Many times, mailbags got shuffled and detained and letters 6, 7, and 8 would arrive before 3, 4, and 5. Without the numbering, the experience was like reading every other chapter of a good book or watching scenes from movies on DVD out of order.

Admittedly, email revolutionized our long distance romance, shrunk the silent canyon of gaping communications between us, and made a mouse my best friend. On trips when email was available to him, daily love bytes from Mark sure sweetened our bitter separations, but paper pushed from a laser printer never replaced a personal letter. I liked knowing *his* hands had held and folded the notepaper. I liked seeing and retracing the curves and angles of *his* handwriting. I liked the hearts and doodles *he* had lovingly sketched in the margins and between the lines. I'd keep his letter in my pocket by day and sleep with it by night until another arrived. Every email evaporated with one click, but a shoe-boxed record of Mark's handwritten devotion to me is neatly stored for my future reference and for our children to read and remember their father's love while he was away from them.

For Richer or for Poorer

Let's face it. No one gets rich serving his country. Even our Commander in Chief is paid less than most high-powered professionals. There is no such thing as time and a half for overtime. Soldiers and sailors are salaried. Their pay scale changes more slowly than molasses moving uphill in January, thanks to ever-changing political platforms and lengthy congressional caucuses.

Somewhere between setting up and settling down in our first apartment, we agreed that, due to his unpredictable presence, I would pay the bills and handle the budget that his E-4 income dictated. Since that first LES (Leave and Earnings Statement), I've struggled with underpayments, overpayments, incorrect BAH, BAS, garnishing of wages, forfeiture of earned leave, DEERS hiccups, and entirely missing paychecks. Most of this happened while my sponsor was away earning more bread and butter.

In any marriage, the topic of finances is about as fun as discussing funeral plans. In a military marriage, the budget falls even further toward the bottom of the list of items to be discussed when all the couple has is a two-minute phone call or a two-day turnaround at home. After trying to discuss some of my monetary concerns with Mark unsuccessfully for a few months, I resorted to calling him at work and asking for a formal appointment. He said he would pencil me in. I arrived punctually, bringing take-out Chinese food, and we chewed on our budget together in the privacy of his office. We even caught ourselves laughing and flirting between bites of lo mein and low bank accounts.

On walks, on dates, and on long drives we've often brainstormed exciting, viable business ideas and have seriously considered civilian entrepreneurship. Our work-days would be shorter; we'd be together; the pay would be much better; we could grow some roots, and we could actually make plans further out than the few weeks in front of us. God always reminds us gently that we are called by Him into this profession of servanthood, that although the grass looks greener, fresher, tastier in other places, our place is with the Shepherd. He will lead us to the best pastures where we can be nourished and can lie down in safety by His side under His watchful care. We would rather have less, live in the palm of His hand, and be held close to His heart than to have more and wander away from Him.

John the Baptist's bottom line to the soldiers by the riverbank was "be content with your pay" (Luke 3:14). Apparently, they, too, struggled with feeling overworked and underpaid. God has promised to "meet all your needs according to his glorious riches in Christ Jesus" (Philippians 4:19). He really does! I haven't had to serve locust and honey casserole, and my children aren't clothed in camel's hair yet. Mark and I are learning, like the apostle Paul did, "to be content whatever the circumstances." We "know what it is to be in need" and we "know what it is to have plenty." We are learning "the secret of being content in any and every situation, whether well fed or hungry, whether living in plenty or in want." We "can do everything through him who gives [us] strength" (Philippians 4:11–13).

In Sickness and in Health

Mark is not the man I married. Today he has a new eardrum; a renovated nose; pins, screws, and cadaver bones in his foot; assorted snaps, crackles, and pops in his back and knees; and a few other rearrangements of body parts that weren't there the day I said "I do." His physically demanding career has pushed his body to its limits and left its mark permanently on his health. Neither am I the woman he married. Time, gravity, age, and our constant pilgrimage around the planet have left their signatures on my body as well.

True, beauty is fleeting, but believe me, it heads for the hills more quickly in this military lifestyle, which is full of physical and emotional stress that the civilian world can only slightly taste along with their salty popcorn at their local movie theaters. All the best health habits in the world can't slow the clock or make our bodies invincible. Sooner or later, sickness and injury knock at our door. Whether it is a case of the sniffles or serious injury or illness, we wives promised with lip-glossed mouths and starry eyes at the altar to hang in there "in sickness and in health," come what may, including premature balding. Regardless of disintegrating vigor and vitality, in God's eyes, our vows remain intact and untouched by the ravages of time.

To Love and to Cherish

It doesn't take long for the warm fuzzies of newly married love to cool and become prickly. That's because real life steps in. In any marriage, but especially in a military marriage, love must run more deeply than the physical senses. Love must live at a deeper level, below what is felt, past what is seen, and beyond what is heard. A woman's love for a military man must pulsate from the very heart, from a place in the soul that neither sees, touches, nor hears anything physical.

Military contracting is huge business. Two parties negotiate at length about A, B, and C, then sign on the dotted line forming a temporary, legal partnership. Marriage is not a contract; it is a covenant. We commit to lifelong, exclusive partnership, *then* work out the negotiables as we go along. A contract is loveless. A covenant is love powered.

Mark and I made a pact years ago to have all our arguments together in the bathtub (they don't last long) and to make our major decisions while strolling through a cemetery (a reminder that only a few things in life truly matter). The end result: love always wins.

"Love is patient" even when workdays are long and homecomings from deployments are delayed. "Love is kind" when frustrations mount and fatigue compounds an already difficult lifestyle of moves, dangers, and separations. "It does not envy" the couples who can celebrate holidays, birthdays, and anniversaries together every year, who live near their extended families, and who have legible address books. "It does not boast, it is not proud" about how much it has over-

Love is the victor in every battle on the home front.

come in the past nor about its plans for the future. "It is not rude" even in self-defense when sorely disappointed by the unexpected or unavoidable. "It is not self-seeking" but is observant at home, at the commissary, and at command functions and works diligently to meet the needs of others. "It is not easily angered" but has learned to trust love's plan over the government's agenda.

154

"It keeps no record of wrongs" and forgives any and all blunders, broken promises, and injuries inflicted to the heart. "Love does not delight in evil but rejoices with the truth" even when the truth means another move, another separation, or even a spouse's infidelity. "It always protects, always trusts" as if it has never been hurt or disappointed before. Love "always hopes, always perseveres. Love never fails" (1 Corinthians 13:4–8). Love is the victor in every battle on the home front.

A Cord of Three Strands

"Mom, will you braid my hair?" When my daughters' own attempts fail, I am the backup beautician in residence. My favorite "do" to coif is the French braid. I like brushing and parting their long tresses to create intricate blonde and golden patterns from their hairlines to their waistlines. I find it challenging and relaxing. Their plaited pigtails please everyone all day long. Altogether, I've hovered over my daughters' heads for hundreds of hours. Over the years, I've probably braided miles of locks. Lots of trial and error have nearly perfected my *plait*-ability. Braiding requires patience. It also requires balance, temperance, and perseverance to intertwine three separate pieces of hair into a crown to top one's crown.

Marriage to a service member requires patience, balance, temperance, and perseverance as well. There must be room for plenty of trial and error to perfect compatibility. Marriage is not a simple, one-time tying of the knot. Marriage that thrives and survives is an untiring, continual braiding of three strands: the husband, the wife, and the Lord. "Though one may be overpowered, two can defend themselves. A cord of three strands is not quickly broken" (Ecclesiastes 4:12). As we continue to put God in the middle, He makes us one. The result is a life crowned with His blessings.

'Til Death Do Us Part

The training, schools, and deployments that separate husbands and wives temporarily are child's play compared to death that separates them for a lifetime. The good-byes said shipside are elementary compared to the final "I love you" whispered bedside. When the "til death do us part" is cued on life's stage, all other farewells fade. We ache for the one left standing on life's pier as the departed drifts away and drops from sight behind the stage curtain. All that remains is faith, hope, and love: the faith that in Christ we will one day see each other again; the hope that all God has promised He will surely do; and the love that was tested, fired, and proven in the kiln of life's joys and pain.

Faith, hope, and love...and sometimes a honey-do list.

My best friend's mother passed away suddenly in the spring of 2001. The grief that followed was intense. In a breath, a husband lost his beloved wife, three children lost their mother, three grandchildren lost their grandmother, and I, like many others, lost a cherished friend.

Eighteen months later I visited Jim, her widower, in their home in Phoenix. I visually browsed the hallway and tabletops, enjoying the gallery of framed photos, old and recent, of their life as man and wife. Some made me laugh; some made me cry, but none affected me as profoundly as a narrow strip of note paper I found taped below the kitchen phone. Phrases written in his wife's penmanship filled the memo. "Clean out the garage," "Service the car," and others were crossed out. "Organize the attic" and others were not. Not knowing she would soon die, one of the last things my friend's mother had done was make a honey-do list for her husband, a compilation of odd jobs that weighed heavily on her mind for which she wanted his help, a gentle register of a wife's requests.

In a beautiful way, her tally of tasks that needed attention played a powerful role in healing her husband's broken heart as he passed through difficult phases of grief. In the months that followed, he worked wholeheartedly to complete the chores. The list whispered echoes of his lover's heart that reverberated through their small house and through the vast void in his life. The last requests of his bride, scribbled and jotted on that paper, and his slow, but steady fulfillment of them kept their hearts close while separated.

The relationship shared by Jesus Christ and His followers is likened to the intimacy a husband shares with his wife. Jesus is called the Bridegroom; the church is His bride (Isaiah 62:5; Revelation 19:6–9). Christ's love for the church is the watermark for all husbandly love (Ephesians 5:25–33). He "was, and is, and is to come" (Revelation 4:8). Until then, He has entrusted to us a honey-do list, the written instructions in His Word that we are to follow while we are separated. His honey-do list provides us the "wait training" we need to become His blemish-free bride. Reading and rereading His honey-do list brings us comfort and knits our hearts together while we wait for Him and ready ourselves for His sure return.

Disciples and Deployments

Jesus's disciples understood the hurt, disappointment, confusion, and pain of being separated from the One they loved. We have stood on piers, on tarmacs, and on beaches and watched our husbands sail or fly into the sunset to undisclosed destinations. The disciples stood atop the Mount of Olives and watched Jesus disappear into the clouds.

> They were looking intently up into the sky as he was going, when suddenly two men dressed in white stood beside them. "Men of Galilee," they said, "why do you stand here looking into the sky? This same Jesus, who has been taken from you into heaven, will come back in the same way you have seen him go into heaven."
>
> —Acts 1:10–11

Therein is the key to a successful marriage, military or not: both partners continually braiding Christ into the center of everything, and then making choices, choosing words and attitudes, and taking actions in the light of the Lord's soon return. While we wait for Him, we prepare ourselves and allow His promised return to transform everything we are.

One fine day, we will suffer no more separations of any kind—deployments, delays, or deaths—from the ones we love. On that day, the grandest marriage ceremony of all eternity will take place. You and I will wear the veil. Jesus Christ, our promised Bridegroom, will meet us at the altar of altars. There will be no more wait training, only togetherness forever. "Let us rejoice and be glad and give him glory! For the wedding of the Lamb has come, and his bride has made herself ready" (Revelation 19:7). Our wedding gift to Him will be the honey-do list with all the items crossed off and well done.

It sounds like a fairy tale, but it is not. It is a true story based on the best-selling Book. Until that day, I make my marriage work by simply following Christ's honey-do list and hiding His numbered love letters addressed to me in the pocket of my heart.

It is not a hope chest crammed with homemaking gear that insures a great marriage. It is a chest with a heart full of hope.

Ideas for Ministry to Military Families

*a*fter a dry invocation, the pastor extended a sappy welcome to the few of us nameless, faceless visitors, who were scattered around the large sanctuary. Suddenly the orchestra flared up on his inconspicuous cue. Violins, trumpets, bass drums, and cymbals reverberated off the altar's ornate stained glass windows and pealed toward the last pew in the balcony's shadows and back again. The blast startled our family, jolting each of us two inches off the bench. Instantly, the drowsy congregation was transformed by the trumpet blast into a Sunday morning Christian version of Disneyland's "It's a Small World." We held tightly to our pew. It had become our stationary boat surrounded by bright-eyed, grinning puppets that robotically turned, nodded, showed some teeth, extended a hand and welcome brochure, and then turned to mechanically greet one another.

During the two-minute "ride" through the labyrinth of smiling church members clad in bright clothes and glittery jewelry, we were serenaded by the choir's rote rendition of "Plenty of Room in the Family." The only thing this church had plenty of room for was improvement. The organ piped its last note and, on cue once more, the congregation settled into their self-assigned cushioned pews and slumped back into their trance, satisfied by their grandioso show of Christian love.

During the church members' halfhearted welcoming display, one middle-aged woman greeted me, silently sizing up my suspicious lack of a husband. Another woman boldly asked, "Is your husband with us today?"

"No, ma'am," I responded. "He's in the service and he's away right now."

She trilled, "Oh! There are many military families in our membership. You'll feel right at home here!" batting her fake eyelashes.

In the still after the storm, my heart ached as I sat between my three fidgety preschoolers. Our growing, mobile family was on the trail again, hunting for the right church at a new duty station. Once more, I was braving the jungle without my partner, children in tow, to find a church home, a home away from home, a family away from family.

After surviving the milquetoast sermon and another flare of a benediction, I led my family down the aisle and out of that church in search of food and rest. No, I don't mean Shoney's and a Sunday afternoon nap. Our hearts were hungry for spiritual food: a genuine welcome, acceptance into a loving family of believers, and morsels of meat from the Word of God with which we could grow strong enough to fight the battles unique to our military life. Our spirits had grown weary from severing friendships at our last home port and by the tensions of transporting our tonnage of belongings and three children across the country. Our spirits needed compassion, restoration, and mending to face the days ahead.

Our spirits needed compassion, restoration, and mending to face the days ahead.

After two decades on the road, we realize the strong need for churches to learn to go beyond recognizing or reaching servicemen and their families at the Fourth of July church musical or briefly on Veteran's Day. Too many congregations, despite the fact that service families live all around them, have very little understanding or insight into the grind of military living. They see the patriotism, the heroism, the red, white, and blue commitment to our great country. They admire the bravery, the honor, the discipline of our soldiers. They may even to some degree appreciate the selflessness and total sacrifice American men and women make to preserve our and our allies' very freedom to peaceably assemble in Christ's name. Their lack of understanding and empathy, however, and more acutely, their lack of a mission outlook and servants' hearts, renders most churches unarmed for helping its military members and families meet and be victorious in the challenges of the military lifestyle.

The role of the church is to deliver the gospel and to equip the saints; thus, these objectives must be at the heart of all ministries. Below are listed many practical ideas for outreach and ministry to military families, most of which can be integrated into existing programs. Some efforts will need to be initiated separately and remain set apart.

For Military Wives

Military wives' support group, fellowship, or Bible study—No one can help a military wife as effectively as the ones who have experienced the realities of military life. Identify the military wives within the local body of believers. Mobilize and assimilate them according to their God-given talents and abilities to serve one another. Inspire this group of women to support and encourage each other on an ongoing basis as care/cell groups within the church and in the community.

Foster families—So often a woman is left alone on Thanksgiving, Christmas, and Easter. Who wants to open a can of turkey soup on Thanksgiving, spend Christmas Day with toddlers and the TV, hide Easter eggs alone, or sing a Happy Birthday solo? Foster families could include military wives and their children during holiday celebrations and on special days. A warm, balanced meal with Christian fellowship on ordinary days is equally a blessing.

Emergency stand-ins—In the event of her own sickness or one of her children's severe illness or hospitalization, a military wife needs a temporary stand-in mom to care for her children in order to get through the crisis. Also, a military wife who works outside the home may, at times, need some type of home repair and can't be home to let the plumber or electrician in the house. When a kitchen socket is powerless or a faucet drips all night, a stand-in to let the repairman in is most appreciated.

Babysitter lists/pools—Finding a gentle, trustworthy sitter is hard enough in one's hometown, let alone a new community. Youth group leaders can offer CPR and advanced babysitting courses at church through the local recreation center or YMCA to train teenage and college-age girls and guys for this ministry. Also, mothers who offer child care in their homes can be included on the list.

Volunteer handymen and handywomen—A pool of willing men and women, talented in areas of home and car repair, would be a godsend for a military wife. These volunteer handypersons would be on call for women whose spouses are deployed and for single mothers, as well. Also, these experts could offer free crash courses in basic auto mechanics, basic home repair, etc., as a ministry to all interested church members.

Ruth and Naomi ministry—Most military wives are hundreds or thousands of miles from their mothers. Young wives could be paired with older women in the congregation to form Ruth/Naomi relationships of love, commitment, prayer, practical support, and advice.

Family doc on call—Inevitably, a child spikes a high fever or gets infested with pinworms on Friday night when all military medical clinics and pharmacies are closed. The bleak weekend suddenly looms ahead, a 60-hour nightmare. A simple call to a willing, licensed church member, for example, an MD, DO, RN, or LPN, could be a tremendous help and relief for a frenzied young mother.

Mother's day out/mom's night out—These programs offer a much-needed break for solo moms who serve children 24 hours a day, seven days a week with no partner. There have been days when I would have paid someone $100 for a half-day break from mommying.

English as a Second Language: classes and tutors— A high percentage of military men have foreign wives who cannot speak or read English. This makes military life for both of them even more difficult. Free courses offered at the church could serve as an instrument for gospel witness as well. One-on-one tutelage could develop into discipling relationships and friendships.

For the Children

Big Brother program—While no one can take Dad's place when he's deployed, father and/or big brother figures are crucial in the lives of military children. Men from youth, single, and married adult departments could volunteer to spend regular time with the children of absentee dads. Monthly group activities, such as baseball games, museum visits, kite flying, and picnics, would facilitate friendships between the big brothers and the children. Mom cannot be Dad all of the time. The male friendship, godly role modeling, and discipling influence of the Big Brothers would be priceless.

Uncle Sam's Kids—This outreach would offer biblically based guidance and loving direction for kids dealing with the adult-size emotions brought on by our splintered way of life. Through games, Bible studies, arts and crafts, and puppet shows, kids of military families would find the comfort and wisdom from God's Word they so desperately need.

Adopt-a-Grandparent program—Volunteer senior citizens could be paired with military families to be "grandpa" and "grandma" to children who rarely see or talk with their grandparents, not to mention have a secure, loving relationship with them. One church we attended presented a musical entitled "Bifocals and Bubble Gum" to kick off such a ministry.

Adopt-a-Service Member program—The members of the child's Sunday school class could "adopt" the child's deployed parent, making and sending cards, care packages, and photographs of their activities.

For the Service Member

Iron sharpens iron—The military world is saturated with opportunities for worldly indulgence. A Christian serviceman experiences tremendous loneliness as he attempts to be "in the world but not of it." With each move and on every deployment, my husband longs for a brother in Christ with whom he can build a lifetime relationship and grow in his faith; someone he can disciple or be discipled by; someone with whom he can pray and share his concerns and fears; someone to whom he can be held accountable for his choices and actions, one-on-one, man-to-man.

Men's prayer breakfasts—Most men's prayer breakfasts are scheduled around 7:00 A.M. or 7:30 A.M., too late for any serviceman to attend and not be UA! Those who plan such fellowships need to be sensitive to a serviceman's work hours, especially if there is a large number of military men in the area.

Making Use of Gifts

These are a few avenues of ministry for reaching those in the military world. It is equally important to stress that members of military families have much *to give* as well. They are rich in talents of teaching, administration, helps, and other gifts which the Holy Spirit gives according to God's purposes. Most military families are masters in the art of hospitality, a skill they have learned over years of moving and making new friends. Programs, such as the ones listed in this chapter, could be coordinated, marketed, and improved upon by military folks. No matter what skills or talents they possess, believers serving in the military have, above all, strength of character and tender hearts—the key to all successful, Christ-centered ministries.

Ministry Contact Information

For additional information, visit
http://www.hopeforthehomefront.com

One Hope Ministry
Phone: 1-757-681-HOPE (1-757-681-4673)
Monday–Friday
9:00 A.M.–5:00 P.M. EST

Personal Letters and Email Welcomed
One Hope Ministry
P. O. Box 1165
Monument, Colorado 80132-1165
USA
marshele.waddell@onehopeministry.com

An Invitation from Jesus

Dear One,

I know you intimately. I love you deeply. I am intensely interested in the details of your life. I am completely aware of the special physical, emotional, and spiritual needs you have as the wife of a serviceman. I, too, am a warrior. The Lord is My name. I, your loving Savior, want to be actively involved in your life.

I leave the first step up to you. Everything in My creation has a first, a beginning. Everybody has a birthday. Every book begins with a first page. Every song begins with a first note. Every journey begins with the first step. Likewise, your search for personal wholeness has a proper beginning.

The first step toward true contentment is entrance into a right relationship with God, through Me, Jesus Christ, His Son. I am the Alpha and the Omega, the Beginning and the End. Believing in Me is the beginning of a right relationship with God. I, God the Son, who existed before time as part of the Holy Trinity, humbled Myself more than 2,000 years ago, became flesh, and lived among mankind.

God's standard of perfection was not within anyone's reach because of sin. Everyone missed the mark, except Me. I lived a perfect life, a life without sin, unlike the rest of men and women. My Father loved *you* so much that He gave Me, His only begotten Son, that whoever believes in Me should not die, but have everlasting life. By dying on the cross, I paid your debt to God that you could never pay. My Father has promised that you can know and enjoy the fullness of His love and His exciting plan for your life if you believe and trust in Me as your one and only Hope. If you choose not to believe, you will one day die and be separated from God forever.

Eternal life is a free gift from My Father for you. Just say with your mouth that I am Lord of your life and believe in your heart that God raised Me from the dead; then you will be saved. I will forgive your sin and remove all your shame, once and for all.

I promise to then give you a new heart and put a new spirit in you. I will remove from you your heart of stone and give you a heart of flesh. I will put My Spirit in you to move you to follow My decrees and be careful to keep My laws.

I am at the door of your heart, knocking. If you hear My voice and open the door, I will come in to you and eat with you, and you with Me. We will have unbroken, unbreakable togetherness forever.

Love,
Jesus Christ

Exodus 15:3; Revelation 1:8; Revelation 22:13; John 3:16; Acts 2:38–39; Romans 3:23; Romans 6:23; Romans 10:9–10; Hebrews 9:26–28; Ezekiel 36:26–27; Revelation 3:20

from Broadman & Holman and New Hope Publishers.

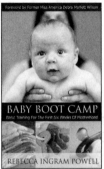

Baby Boot Camp
*Basic Training for the First
Six Weeks of Motherhood*
Rebecca Ingram Powell
ISBN 1-56309-820-2

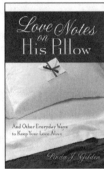

Love Notes on His Pillow
*And Other Everyday Ways
to Keep Your Love Alive*
Linda J. Gilden
ISBN 1-59669-014-3

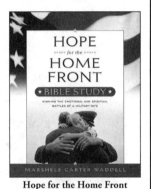

**Hope for the Home Front
Bible Study**
*Winning the Emotional and
Spiritual Battles of a Military Wife*
Marshéle Carter Waddell
ISBN 1-59669-033-X

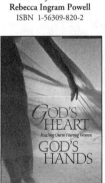

God's Heart, God's Hands
*Reaching Out
to Hurting Women*
Denise George
ISBN 1-56309-831-8

A Whisper in Winter
*Stories of Hearing God's Voice
in Every Season of Life*
Shannon Woodward
ISBN 1-56309-823-7

Refuge
*A Pathway Out of Domestic
Violence and Abuse*
Detective Sergeant Donald Stewart
ISBN 1-56309-811-3

new
hope
PUBLISHERS

Available in bookstores everywhere. www.newhopepublishers.com

New Hope® Publishers is a division of WMU®,
an international organization that challenges Christian
believers to understand and be radically involved in
God's mission. For more information about WMU,
go to www.wmu.com. More information
about New Hope books may be found at
www.newhopepublishers.com. New Hope books
may be purchased at your local bookstore.